A Cowboy's Thoughts

Looking Back

By

Merle Roehr

1663 LIBERTY DRIVE, SUITE 200
BLOOMINGTON, INDIANA 47403
(800) 839-8640
WWW.AUTHORHOUSE.COM

© 2005 Merle Roehr. All Rights Reserved.

No part of this book may be reproduced, stored in a retrieval system, or transmitted by any means without the written permission of the author.

First published by AuthorHouse 01/12/05

ISBN: 1-4208-1958-5 (sc)

Printed in the United States of America
Bloomington, Indiana

This book is printed on acid-free paper.

All photography by Merle Roehr

Dedication and Thanks

I am forever indebted to my father, Richard Roehr and my grandfather, Chester Roehr. Without their influence on me, I would have never experienced the enjoyment of being a cowboy. The life they have lived made me dream of one day being able to live a small part of it.

I also am indebted to Ervin (George) McDainiel. It was his influence and death which started me writing and remembering those things which molded my life. To each of these men I owe much gratitude.

I would now like to thank my wife, Annette. She spent many hours on the computer so my stories would be on disk. She also spent many hours convincing me to put them into book form; she believed others would enjoy them. Without her support and love, it would have never happened.

Preface

Sometimes there is an agony that comes from deep within a man that wants to escape. There seems to be a necessity to be in another time, a time when men were free spirits, somewhere in the west a hundred years ago. The longing for the kind of life that has no boundary.

One of sitting behind a loose rein or at the edge of a small campfire, and the romance that we all attribute to that way of life. One thing I know this man cannot escape this agony except through the pen.

Introduction

As a cowboy and one who appreciates this style of poetry or storytelling and is a believer in God, there are some parallels that can be drawn between the life, the culture, and the work of a cowboy and the truth of which the Bible speaks. It may be of little interest or thought to any, who do not understand who a cowboy is or what they stand for. I will be the first to say that not all have the same values, but there are a great many who are good, God-fearing men.

We watch too much television, we believe that all men who live the lifestyle of a cowboy must be living a life without God. We need to know, that all walks of life have those living within them who live as if there were no accountability for their actions. It does not mean those lifestyles are void of men who know God. The cowboy that is a follower of Christ has a unique picture of God and His creation. Maybe through some of the stories and poems, there will be something you can grasp and seek to find God or give you the encouragement to stay with Him.

Between the years 2001 and 2004, I have spent many hours in thought, simply about a way of life. I would never claim to be an authority, philosopher, nor a great writer. I do, however, believe I am a man who enjoys a way of life and hope I can share it with others. Some of these stories are for fun, some make a very good point, but they are all for your pleasure. Hope you enjoy.

Frosted Mornin

Last Walk With A Friend
In memory of Ervin (George) McDaniel

I think of myself as a cowboy of modern time, maybe somewhat misplaced and misunderstood at times. We often do not have anyone who cares or wants to, but on rare occasions there comes one who just fills that place. It is not often that any of us have close friends, with the same joys, pleasures, and thoughts as we do. Ervin was that man, one I can still call a friend. They pass through our lives, and in passing they leave a great empty space, great lasting memories and dreams. They will always be missed. This is about one of these men.

I was there that day to reminisce of the times we had and to plan those in the future, of things we would do together, of things we would never do. There were hopes and dreams and the joys of life, not living, but life itself, one of which no man could quench. He was a man of seventy-three years, thirty my senior, with whom I had the pleasure to share part of that life and dreams. He was one I still counted as a true friend. He had recently had open heart surgery and with it there was a weakness, physically. We did not care to look at the shortness of life. Nevertheless, it was there. What I did see was his heart for adventure and for life was still strong. That which brought us together, were children and horses and the pleasure of them both, the later of which we were enjoying in that hour.

The afternoon was hot and muggy, but exercise had been prescribed and he had not yet accomplished it for the day. He usually walked the drive in front of the house with his wife each day. This day was an exception, this was a day for visiting and he had part of a dream and his life he wished to share with me. There was a horse, or for that matter several horses, all pleasure horses. One he had bought to ride, the others simply to look at. Beautiful to look at as horse flesh? Not necessarily, they were Mustang or crossbred and some just old, but all the same, pleasure. We walked back through the old improvements, under some big old oak trees. The trees were some fair symbols of life. They too showed wear and tear, but were still full of life. We crossed a small tank dam. Fresh rains had caused the water therein. We enjoyed the water. We talked of the life it would bring to the garden, trees, and stock. We remarked about the small washes in the red clay that the rain had left. The mark left by the rain may have been a harsh mark, but in passing small clumps of grass would take over, a beginning. We continued up the hill, the full distance was maybe two hundred yards, but it was slow and enjoyable. We reminisced, we looked at that which was around us, we seemed to forget the hot, sticky air around us. We arrived at the top, there were two old discarded tractor tires, discarded as trash, used up and useless. The tires no matter how useless were under a small tree, a place to find comfort and rest. From this point, we could see most of the pasture, and call for the horses. In waiting, we continued our visit, but most of all just being friends. We saw the horses, talked of each, and enjoyed the pleasure that each of us found in them. The horses were taken to the barn. There I saddled the big horse for him. Ervin's health would not permit him the pleasure of riding, but he wished to receive pleasure through my riding and to share that pleasure with our families and me. The day would have been considered quite uneventful in most people's eyes. It was simply friendship.

The evening was growing late. We said our goodbyes for the night, knowing that it could be our last goodbye. It was three days later I was called, I was told of his passing, the evening before.

I will miss him, there is an empty place, one washed out. There is one thing I know, every time I see a horse, every time I saddle mine, even when feeding, I will remember Ervin. The friendship and pleasures we had, I hope I can share them with someone else. I knew him five years. I cannot know how many friends he must have shared within that seventy-three years. I just hope they can remember him in the same way.

> A hot fire, hot pot of coffee,
> good friends with warm hearts,
> what more ought be ask for.

Going Back

These are times of nostalgia, something I have tried to live in most of my life. Often our past is the hardest thing to leave behind. Most likely it is the reason I write things like this.

Living in the past is where I most want to be.
Things all remembered are good memories.

If we continue to live pleasures of the past.
The pleasures of the future never will last.

If we long to always look back.
We will never see a future to look back at.

If we dwell on our future.
There is no reason for our past.

Too many live only for their future success.
Others look back only to see their failures.

A Cowboy's Thoughts

If we have refused to live in our future.
There are no memories to make the past,
where we want to be.

If I had known the trials of the future.
I would have paid more attention to the present.
Sometimes the memories are all we have.

Change

The man that does not need change,
He is the perfect man.
The man who does not change,
He is the same as dead.
That man who wants to change,
He is looking for life.
That man who will change,
He has life.

Never pass up a chance to do something,
even if it's something you might not like,
as long as it's not morally wrong.
Experience is a wonderful thing.

Cowboy Dreams

We're a long way from those days when men were free to wander on a horse back. When men could see the sunset every evening and awake to the sunrise each morning. Some were born a hundred years too late, in places where buildings are much too tall and the skies are much too gray. With all those days too much passed.

There are those rare times we see a sunset or a sunrise or maybe even a clear, blue, open sky with small puffs of pure, white clouds in the distance. We are all allowed to dream for a short time. To reflect on things we could have seen in that time.

The cold crisp morning air, a cold saddle, the horse's cold back, or a short snort as the rigging slaps your horse's back. To hear the creak of the saddle and see the steam from the mount's nose. To drop of the edge of the cap-rock, to smell the sweat, the frost, and the strong aroma of the sage and cedar that are visible all around. Everywhere I look there is the beauty that the cowboy must have seen a hundred years ago. I see the cattle gather as others push them from the breaks and the brush into the clearing. There is the smokey smell of a freshly started branding fire and the coffee from the wagon. There is the pleasurable thought of warmth, then I realize the cold I feel. Later there is the bawl of freshly branded calves, split from their mamas. The feel of the rope as it slides through my hand. The smell of burning hair. The yelling, the moving around of the herd, the calling of my name. Someone needs help! I have become one of them. Then I realize that I am being called, but not in the dream, it is for real. I am pulled back through that reality of time. But for just a little while I have been able to dream, to lighten the load, and forget the fast pace world I was born into. Just a hundred years too late!

A Cowboy's Thoughts

There's not many a person,
with all their ideas and whims.
Who will ever come close,
to where the cowboy's thoughts begin.

It's somewhere back in the past,
or somewhere out in the wide-open west

It could be in a dry crusted desert.
It could be on a snow crested mountain
On the Mexican border
or out on the coast.

He could be walking the streets in his boots.
He could be on his trusted cayuse

You can bet their thoughts are all the same.
And all would stand, and fight their claim.

I could start to describe and draw out their plan.
But you'll never know the thought of the man.

Merle Roehr

> You might stay around and play the part.
> But you never can pry it out of his heart.

A Cowboy's Thoughts

Time for Cow Work

Merle Roehr

Visible Signs of Real Cow Work

These observations are not that of just a cowboy but of a cowhand. If you come into headquarters, line camp or up to the wagon and you see any number of these things, you are around a real cow working camp and in good company.

Boots with holes in em, saddles with slick spots,
spliced reins,
worn, cracked leggings, spurs without silver that shine,
wet blankets, lathered horses, limbered ropes.
Sweated and stained hats, unsettled dust.

Digger blades worn thin as cigarette paper,
fresh tamped dirt, new cedar post and new barbed wire,
fresh mesquite grubs, newly burned pasture, black
windmill oil.
Callused hands, dark leathery skin
and busted knuckles.

Baby calves in the heifer pasture,
branding fires still burning, bloody hocked calves,
burned out branding irons, swinging beef,

empty Bull Durham sacks and long shadows.
A cowboy with a smile on his face,
a cup of black coffee.

You see even though the work is hard and dirty, there are enjoyable pleasures, accomplishments and relaxation. Every day is different and the scenery always changes. You see, it's the place some of us want to be.

Merle Roehr

Little Cowboy

Cowboys and Lollipops

I often have thoughts considered a little odd. There is one question that has come to mind. "Why are cowboys called cowboys?" No, why do we use the word boys? There are several things that have brought this question to mind. The most prevalent is the opinion the public has of cowboys. There are many things that have tainted the eye of the public, most often the television or those who think the cowboy indicate a style, as it seems to today. We think of the man who is out on the ranch, the tall slender old man, whose skin is like leather. We then seem to go to another extreme, those who are drunken, immoral men who are incapable of doing anything else. There are so many preconceived ideas that we sometimes miss the point, although the previous ideas do take place, I believe, we should look at the other side of things and see the whole story.

The answer to the question, "why are cowboys called cowboys?" Well it could be that most of them started as boys. Those who made the trail drives, would have had some older men among them for guidance. For example, the trail boss, a foreman, the cook, and maybe even the man who owned the cattle, but the larger portion of the crew would have to be young. To start with the country was young and full of risk and those who were of any age had just finished the Civil War. They were finished with that type risk. Many had families, many had just started a new life in a new country, and many had died in that war. The other reason was the boys were looking for a better way of life, with all the romance and excitement that had come to their ears. They were boys who were willing to put in a full day of men's work, and then some. Nevertheless, the adventure was still there. These boys were full of excitement, orneriness and exuberance. They were simply full of life and able to endure the pains that older men had grown full of.

One of the things that brings me to this point, are stories that the old timers have told over the years. My dad has told that in 1949 he was thirteen. He had watched two young men break the rough string that year and while they worked they taught him how to do the job. The next year the JA Ranch hired him to break the rough string. This was all brought to mind again when I saw a young man I knew. It was early morning and they had stopped for gas and a snack. He introduced me to his two sons and a friend of theirs, none over fourteen, all were decked out for cow work, their horses saddled and ready for work. You would have seen them appear as men. A short time later I entered the station and all these boys were leaned over the counter, spurs dangling, digging through ten gallons of lollipops. They headed back to the pickup laughing and joking, it seemed that those lollipops were their biggest prizes.

I don't intend to remove the old picture of the cowboy, only give you another to look at. At this age I'm not as limber or agile, things don't happen as easy. The day will come for them also. Someday some younger boys will take their place. I just hope young cowboys always have lollipops.

A Cowboy's Thoughts

Cowboys and Lollipops

There in front of that old store
Their horses were tied, they head for the door
Their paw introduced them, tall and proud
Their attire-hollered cowboy, right out loud

I knew their paw, he'd work em hard
They would fill the part, and never show tard
You might look at em, and think em men
The next time you would see em it might be pretend

But with all the exuberance and boyish play
You could plant em on a horse and know they'd stay
You could see through the window their hand in a jar
But when it comes down to business they wouldn't be far

Here they come out the door
With lollipops in hand
But when they get on that horse
They'll all be a man

> He who seeks rest in himself
> will be eternally wanting.
> He who seeks it in God
> will be rested eternally.

I Once Saw a Dead Man

Nothing brings fear or a faint heart to one's being more than that of seeing unnecessary death. The man was a prominent citizen in a small town. He had been missing for a week when his father reported it. Seemed no one else really cared the wife or children had not even mentioned the disappearance. The law looked, but the country is big and rough, some places still hard to get to especially at that time of year, and besides it seemed not many were too concerned. His family was physically well cared for in his life. They all had extra fine cars and the home was well over the million-dollar mark.

It was on a bright day. Three weeks down the road when a law officer called it in. He had been found just three hundred yards off the pavement, down an old dirt road under the edge of a hill. There he lay slumped over on the passenger side floor of a nice rig, with his head under his body. In the seat was an empty bottle of whiskey and another half gone in his hand. Dead from an overdose of whiskey and no air. Those bottles could have been worth a thousand dollars each, but he was still just as dead.

No one cared except the gawkers, It was only their morbid curiosity, and the law that cared for the body. I didn't want to see, maybe that's why they ask me to keep the others back. I watched as they removed the body out of that expensive rig, he was cold, black, swollen, and dead. I thought to myself, what a waste. To me he had everything, a beautiful wife, two children, a big house, nice cars, and what I thought to be all the money in the world.

The one thing he seemed to not have was, someone. No one seemed to care, It was odd, the only thing that mattered to the family was gone when he died, his money.

Did you ever wonder why? Gives you something to think about.

I Once Saw a Dead Man

The man laid there lonesome and cold,
a man of importance, so we are told
he was reported missing at seven days,
Not many concerned, it was just a phase.
It was said he would leave at times for days.

Now it was fourteen days and was quite a concern,
there were many things that needed to be learned
Nothing was there not even a trace.
The law though they looked, there was no case.

At twenty-one days the call came in,
the officer said "we could use some good men."
When we arrived wasn't much we could do,
just keep back the crowd, a gawking they stood.

No one cared for twenty-one days
but they gathered there, now their eyes all a gaze.

Merle Roehr

> All that there was, there to see
> was a dead man and his whiskey.
> He lived his life fast
> and his death came briskly.

I would never make fun of this man's life or death, for life is precious and unnecessary death is such a waste. Had his passion for real life matched his passion for whiskey, there would have been no need to drink. What might he have done?

Her Color of Choice Barn Red

It was to the ranch we moved.
I was happy to live my life anew.
Now there was to my surprise,
A house all painted the shade barn red.
But to my elated self it seemed,
she cared to be somewhere else instead

I knew somehow if time allowed,
she would love the life we lead.
For there's a pull to a way of life,
when in the house you live's barn red.

Now time has passed and we've moved on
our lives have passed like a flash.

We've moved on out,farther west,
to live a life at it's best.
With many a child put in our home,
It is with this we're blessed.

Now we turn down that drive
and there to our surprise,
a barn red house once again
there to enter our lives.

So as time passed by,
how our lives have thrived.

Things were going,as all had planned.
But as always things will change.
It's been in the life we've lead.
We were told that we must move
on over to a brand new spread.

Now it was known then and there
that her conversion was true,
when at her demand it was said
there must be a house barn red.

Now her bed room is mauve
and her sitting room blue.
her horse and her hair are red.
But the picnic table, dog house,
and even the shed, are painted
the shade of barn red.

Now they call us
The Rowdy Red Roehr Ranch.
And we're happy with the life we've lead.

A Cowboy's Thoughts

So the color of choice
through all the years
has always been
the shade, barn red.

Merle Roehr

From Embers to Flames

This is written from the heart of a man who believes that nothing is more important than the love of God and the love a man has for Him. But as for this man, after this, that love of a good woman is placed above all else, including himself.

Of Women and Fire

Women and fire,
are quite the same.

Both are passionate
and filled with flame.

Fire warms the body,
and women the soul.
But both can leave you
alone, lost and cold.

But kindled, nurtured
and handled with care.
There will be an ember,
deep down in there.

Merle Roehr

> If from down in the midst
> can be brought out bold.
> There is a passion within
> which is to behold.

Never let fate take it's course,
it is not worth the time it wastes.

The Old Cowboy

The old cowboy was now past his prime.
The young men thought they were buying him time.

He was close to a century old by now.
Ol man time, had passed him by somehow.

He had ask for a good young horse to ride.
Now what they brought him, was just an old hide.

He gave them a mighty hard chidin,
for this old gray nag he wasn't ridin.

He stood his ground refused the hide,
until the boys brought a real ride.

A nice young red horse, to him they brought.
He mounted up without ne'er a thought.

There seemed to be a silence now.
The young men there, were all waitin for pow.

Merle Roehr

> When the little red horse decided to bust into,
> in all directions the dust and hair flew.
> The old cowboy's spurs, were rakin hair.
> Those long leather reins, were cuttin air.
>
> When the dust and the hair had all cleared,
> the old cowboy still in the saddle quite revered
>
> To retirement all old we might send,
> but he a true cowboy, will remain to the end.

I have found that at many times I am exhausted. I have spent a great deal of these times in an ill mood. In these times I have discovered, I can be exhausted, and in an ill mood and miserable for a long time after. Or I can be exhausted and enjoy the time. We can rest when there is time, and there will be! The latter, always without fail, is more enjoyable, and it works to benefit others and me.

I have often wondered what that cowboy saw on those nights he wandered the prairies, mountains, and deserts, as he roamed free as most of us wish we could.

Wondering Cowboy

Out there in the night so bright.
With all those stars to bring us light.

Those celestial bodies all a glare,
for all of us men just to stare.

We take for granted all the fare.
We seem to forget without a care.

Now the beauty there oh so rare.
Suppose,
God placed it to remind us He's there.

Merle Roehr

The Slicker

It was a bronc ridin open to all.
The prize to be won, it wasn't to small.
They were all rough and ready, awaitin their call.

Then spied someone a dude, all slicked by the city.
And no one there would show any pity.

They laughed and they roared at the slicker's dress.
The long hair topped with derby, he didn't impress.

He was long and lean, not much it seemed.
Being a bronc rider is what he deemed.

The saddle he carried worn and rough.
The spurs he wore blunt and scuffed.

That should have been a clue, but all were confused.
The slicker never stewed the others only mused.

By himself he waited much like the rest.
And all the time he pondered at giving it his best.

A Cowboy's Thoughts

Now each man was called as his bronc came up.
So the slicker sat quietly without even a lump.

When finally he was called, to his bronc he strode.
He throwed on his saddle tightin the load.

Feet in the stirrups set tight in the seat.
He hollered turn him loose! His mind was complete.
He marked him and spurred him that wild old cayuse.
And when he was finished he just turned him loose.

Now as he walked back, he did so with pride.
For he knew the top prize was to ride the ol hide

When the slicker was finished, he gave counsel in part.
A cowboy's not proven by what he might wear,
but proven by what's in his heart

Folks, I am not much bronc rider,
but there is one thing I have learned.
You can be a pretty good bronc rider,
if the saddle,
is more comfortable than the landing.

Merle Roehr

Settin Camp

There are many things that are missed
if with the cow camp you've stayed.
There are yet those things that are sometimes hard
and often leave you dismayed.

There's always good grub,
and most always good mounts.
But there's never a hot tub,
and most always short on count.

When the weathers hot
your always sweatin.
And when the weathers cold
it's always freshenin.

The scenery always at the top of the list.
The quite is always peaceful and crisp.

There is always something different.
There's never a boring minute.
All in all an experience enjoyed.

A Cowboy's Thoughts

The nights are long and cool.
And on what you sleep often rules.

And I wouldn't mind the settin camp strains.
If old men's bones, stood early morn pains.

Merle Roehr

The Belled Horse

A Cowboy's Thoughts

We Belled the Horse

There's a lot of land
away out here.
Seems you just can't feed
the horses too near.
Oh the sky is always
big and clear.
But the chances of showers
are dark and drear.
To turn horses out
brings only fear.
We've wondered how
to keep them here.
We hold their presence
oh so dear.
And so a bell
we added to gear.
We belled the ol gray horse,
so now we hear him far and near.
We slung it round his ol neck,
cause we couldn't tie it to his rear.

Merle Roehr

Ode to Woes

Come and let me tell you a tale
an awful tale of woes.

The longer I look the worse they get,
that's often the way it goes.

The list is long and often cruel
worse than anyone knows.

But I'm going to tell you anyway
for I like the way they'll grow.

Oh the woes ne'er, e'er go away,
for it's the game we like to play.

We all love sympathy, some more than others. The one thing I know, if we are looking for it, big or small it's never good. Life has always, is always, and will always be work and the more I feel sorry for myself the worse it becomes.

I grew up reading a cowboy calender about a poor ol cowhand. Always humorous, but sometimes too close to home. It was always about hard times and often truthful about laziness, and the work it produces. Needless to say, working a ranch takes work and mostly hard work. I have also noticed the less willing we are, the more work there is. One other thing, the more we worry about it, the less we do. Always thinking somebody else should do it.

Merle Roehr

Cowboy Somebody
or Cowboy Woes

The horse I'm ridin is missing some shoes,
right front, left rear.
He might not be quite so cross,
if somebody'd yank the others off.
The cows and calves, are in with another man's bull.
He's a horrible sight to see
The calf crop next spring won't bring ten cents,
if somebody don't fix, that ol fence
The water is short and the tanks are baked
and the mill just aint keeping up
I'm afraid, it's goin bone dry,
if somebody don't start that old pump
I've calves that need branded, bills that need paying,
the wheats not quite keeping up
The horses need worming, the oats need cutting,
and water gaps need putting up
I really don't know how it'll all get done,
but somebody's got work to wind up.

A Cowboy's Thoughts

Old Relic

Merle Roehr

Windmill Wonderings

There are just a few things I can say about windmills. I spent several years working for a pump service company in West Texas, and a good third of our business was the windmill. After that I spent several years on the ranch and cared for about forty mills the year around.

They are cantankerous, man killing creatures, maybe built to antagonize cowboys and wind millers. Yet all in all I still find myself drawn to them. They are becoming a relic remembered, simply put one of the last ghosts of the past. Unless you have needed water in the worst way and a mill has been down, you might not understand the important role they played in settling the west. Simply put, for all the trouble they are, I am still in love with them.There are many fond memories of the mills I have worked on, and those I have lived with. On the ranch there have been just a few of them! I believe mills are one of the most relaxing things I've been around.

There was one mill I remember most, for some reason as much work as it took, it has always given memories of pleasure. When I found the mill, it had been down for four years and in much disarray. It was high on a hill below the cap-rock between a large draw and the river. I spent several days rebuilding it and when it was set to pumping the checks sang and pumped water with ease. The water the old mill pumped was as cool and sweet as any on the place. It was enjoyable to sit at the base of the mill, close my eyes and just listen. Later I did just this when I had the time. I would just sit there and listen to those check's rattle. On spring days the old bull frogs would croak and a steady stream of water would pour into that old dirt tank. The cattails grew thick around the edge of the tank. The orange winged starlings could be seen standing almost sideways on the stems, giving that distinct whistle. Sometimes I would just watch the water bugs skimming on that clear water, or the little groups of tadpoles darting back and forth. Sometimes early of a morn I could catch the deer come to water, or maybe watch the small coons play at the edge. Whatever the occasion, being there at the mill always made my day go better.

Merle Roehr

She's a Gracious Old Relic

Clangin, clatterin, sweekin, squalkin
that old rattlin relic set loose on that hill.

An old crown of blades jagged and torn,
an old bonnet oily and worn.

A little breeze rocked that old wheel,
but the load on the rod brought it to yield.

It seemed to say I'm old and tired,
but that West Texas wind was gonna get hard.

The sun was high when that ol wind got up
then that ol mill started to pump.

She wern't much to look at there standing alone,
but she gave up water without even a groan.

She's not in good shape wind millers have told,
but the water she pumps is a sight to behold

Water

Water, water the great substance of life.
Without it there are many a strife.

A substance of rest.
A substance of stress.

Windmills, lakes, streams, and dirt tanks.
Most, always used without any thanks.

But the cowhand that works it, he understands.
All that it takes to make water stand.
The thankfulness, hard work, and all of the plans.

But in all the work and all the stress.
In all the time, through all the rest.

He knows they are useless without moisture falls.
There is always a must that on God he calls.

Merle Roehr

Things I've Learned # 1

Remember that in the barnyard,
the rooster that crows the loudest,
is usually the one with the most to hide.

This might be a good idea to think upon
when deciding weather to open our mouth in
a discussion regarding our own abilities.

As I grow older I have found,
I learn much more
if I keep my ears and mind more open
and my mouth more shut.
Question is why can't I keep it shut?

One thing I've learned in life.
You don't know who a person is,
until you know them.

Everyday life is full of surprises and opportunities,
We just fail to see them.

A Cowboy's Thoughts

The most enjoyment most of us can receive out of life.
Quit living someone else's.

It's not the situation that we live in that's boring,
it is usually us.

There's not much that calms a man's thoughts,
better than a hard day's work and a good night's sleep.

Life seems to be a rough ol go,
but if it were easy
enjoyment would be minimal.
Life is about walking on the edge,
no matter what your profession.

Life is full of difficulties.
We decide whether we will let them get us down,
or if we will work through them and get on with life.

The mood I am in is not the fault of anyone else,
nor is it something I am born with.
I am given the ability to change it and it is my choice to
make it.

It is not that things around us do not affect us,
those things are a part of our life.
The thing we must understand is,
it is always a man's decision,
to do what he does
and be who he is.

If you carry a club,
make sure you can take the beating.

The lack of passion in one's life,
leads only to a lack of life.

Fantasies of Life

Merle Roehr

Thought on Society

We live in a society now, from whence came a set of rules and goals. Those that are not true, nor or they standing solid on anything, They are based on nothing more than what would be seen as personal interest, goals and selfishness. They are running rampant. Worst of all we are willing to let them destroy, in all facets of life. We live our lives on those things which we feel produce happiness in our lives. We condemn all things that have the ability to build joy in our lives, and in others. It seems to be about possessions and power, instead of contentedness and submission. Our ability to grasp reality and see clear pictures is clouded. They are covered by the fantasies of a life of ease and perfectness, in monies and dreams. Those of which we cannot ever pursue, not because dreams are not useful in our lives. It is because they are not based in the reality of the evidence of that one Devine being, God. We look to build kingdoms and pleasures that surpass all our abilities. This is simply because, our appetites are insatiable for things that produce only more appetite.

A Cowboy's Thoughts

Success should not be measured
by what one gains for themselves,
but what one gives to others.

Merle Roehr

A Cowboy's Prayer

All Mighty Lord, we ask that You be with us this day. That each loop thrown might lay square on a set of horns or pickup a set of heels. That each rope might be tied hard or that each dally might be true and not slip. We ask that the rains fall right for tank water and green grass. That the calves come head first and healthy, that the markets are good when they sell. Most of all Lord we thank You for all that You have sent, and if nothing more comes, we would still know that you are a gracious God. We ask that You be with us, that we might keep our mouths and our lives pure, so that others might know we are Yours and that we might show them what we see and know. In Your Son's most Holy Name
    Amen

Don't make light of what
God has given,
He could let it be removed.

A Cowboy's Thoughts

Cowboy's Tack

Merle Roehr

> A merciful God,
> a gentle horse,
> and a good dog.
> What more could a cowboy need.

A Cowboy's Tack

These are the tools that a cowboy uses. The saddle, his boots, a pair of leggings, a pair of spurs, the bits, soft gloves, the hat, a lariat, the blanket or pad, and most of all a trusted horse. If you use your tools and use them well, they will serve you in the work you do. If you look at them and their function, then apply them to your Christian life, it might "just might" help you ride for the brand of Christ

The Saddle - It's the ultimate in a horse being submissive to that one in control. It is in essence, the place in which the master takes control. It reminds me that God sets on that throne in heaven and He is my Lord and Master. My King. I must be submissive.

My Boots - They are handmade by those who understand me, the work I do, and the specialties that I need. They are of the best leather, thick and tough, they withstand the elements they were built for. They fit me to a tee. They help me stand firm, a foundation. They remind me of the foundation laid for me, in every aspect of life. The words given to us in the Bible. They are the Christian's foundation. They fit us to a tee.

The Leggings - They are of heavy leather, protection for my legs. They keep the cold out and the thorny abusive brush from getting under my skin. They are a must, for you have to work through it, to obtain the goal that has been set before you. This reminds me of prayer and the Holy Spirit. We need to pray for protection from the fiery darts of Satan and the ability to see where it is given. Jesus said He would send a Comforter in times of trial. He is always there, if not it is because we left Him.

My Spurs - Some folks may think they're harsh, but we need only to be gentle, if the horse trust, a nudge of encouragement is all that is needed. Their nudge is an urge to continue in adversities. When the brush is too thick, the mountains too steep, or the canyon too deep. This reminds me of the words of Jesus, and the encouragement of Christian brothers and sisters. They are always there in times of need. A kind gentle word of encouragement is sometimes all it takes to continue.

The Bits - They are used to direct the movement of the horse, and to remind him that man has total control. To move in the direction needed, or to simply hold up and to look for what is needed to continue. This reminds me that I am to be submissive to God in all that I do. The idea, is that through His Word there are direction and instruction, it gives us what we need to obtain that gift He has given us, and to lead others in that direction.

The Soft Gloves - They are a comfort to some, they are the protection that softens the harshness of the weather or work. The glove may even soften the touch, in a way of gentleness or giving us the idea of soft gentle hands. These remind me of the gentleness and patience of God. When I stray, the willingness to forgive, if only I repent and ask for it.

The Hat - It shades me, protects me from the sun that beats down on those hot days in the saddle. It reminds me of the time God made a gourd vine to grow up over night to protect Jonah from the sun. Sometimes we have those physical hurts, and we need to know that God also takes care of us in those times.

The Lariat - Ropes are an item that when used correctly, keeps the herd together, healthy, and safe. With the idea of roping strays to bring them back in the herd, or taking down one that is sick and in need of attention, or taking out one that might bring harm to others. I am reminded here that there are those who need to be drawn into God's herd (that is to teach and to convert others to Christ). To help all who are spiritually sick, trying not to lose any, always remembering there are those who teach falsely and must be separated from the herd. In all I am to seek, teach, admonish, touch, and to help those who are in need with the kindness of Christ.

The Blanket or Pad - This the protection from the burden of the load which is carried on the saddle of submissiveness. This submissiveness would be unbearable without it. This reminds me of the love of God and His Son's death on the cross, and His resurrection. Without whom our burdens would be unbearable.

The Horse - The last but not least, they carry that burden without just reward, with forgiveness, in places we could not or would not go. With him we can and do, we call him a beast of burden. This reminds me that there is a Christ always, especially when I am down or tired or just giving up. He is always there carrying the load as long as I am willing to give it to Him. To continue ever so graciously, picking us up, and giving us hope. There are no rewards asked for and forgiveness is always there. I am reminded all too vividly of the burden of the cross He carried until He could no more, and the man who helped Him physically. We should help others when it is at all possible, without being told. I also remembered the sins He carried, those that were yours and mine, a load that is impossible for us to carry. He was, is, and will always be there to make the way for each of us to be children of God. He never asks for reward except that we come to the Father.

> Folks, I love who I am.
> I long to go back to a way of life,
> I have known.
> I never wish to return,
> to the state of life I have lived in.

Merle Roehr

The Ranch and The Kingdom

As a cow hand I'm not the one who always rides or the one who works the stock. I'm the one who takes care of the herd, and not as most folks think. I care for the herd in all aspects. I am the one who opens the gates, nursemaids orphan calves, repairs the fences or windmills. I even patch the water tanks, I can grow feed, prepare it for storage, load and even feed it. I care for stock when it is sick and seek that which is lost. Mine is a life of a working cowboy. I dream of owning a ranch of my own, but my place is that of care.Much like the Kingdom of God, my place is not that of a ruler. It is a place of work, that constant practice of being in the likeness of Christ. I am here to work and care for that which God has intrusted to me. To care for and to seek those which are lost. Always feeding, restoring, and mending souls for He who is our Ultimate Boss.

Truth cannot be accepted as such,
just because it is what we wish to hear.
It must be found to be so,
after much scrutiny.

If it is not scrutinized,
before we repeat it.
Then it becomes nothing more than gossip.

A wise man doesn't tell a story,
until he knows the whole of the story.
And it seems, we are most often
better off, not knowing the second half.

Merle Roehr

Babe

I have a mare. She's not much to look at by some's standards, no papers to prove her breed. She's told to be half paint and half mustang. She's rough to look at and oft times ill natured. She took a plug from my arm one day, the one that combs and curries and even feeds her. Some would say she's not worth the worry to break or the feed to fatten. Yet somewhere between her ears there is a brain, and somewhere in her girth there is a heart, with a walk like a cat and the wit to match. With patience and work, somewhere there is a trust that will be true. With the two of us there's not anything we can't do.

Within this thought, there is a lesson. Me, I'm just a cowboy, not much by some's standards. I have no papers to prove me, no contest I've won. Just hard ranch work I've done. Many a wrong I've made, many an ill streak I've showed. Somewhere between my ears there is a brain, and somewhere in my chest there is a heart, and somewhere in there God put a soul. With all His patience and work there is a trust that is true. Just as that mare looked useless, there was good there, no matter the visible picture, we are all worth something to God. It takes a lot of work to dig it out of all of us. I took the risk of hoofs and teeth because I looked inside that mare, and found the things she was made of. God asked his Son to die on a cross. He knew man would sin and need forgiveness, He knew what man was worth and He will never give up.

Merle Roehr

Trust

All old cowhands should know what true trust is. God asks us to have faith in Him, and place our trust in His hands, yet we all have a problem in turning lose and placing ourselves into His hands. In my mind, we all know what trust is, if we have pulled shoes or picked the spines of a prickly pear from around the hoof of a horse. We have placed trust in that horse, and if he has not kicked us by now he has placed a trust in us. Let us take it a step farther. I've ridden over rough country in the Panhandle of Texas, the lower part of the Palo Duro Canyons, not as bad as some, but worse than most. I have noticed that between horse and rider there is a trust between two beings that is unmatched in most things. The idea is to take a horse and step off a blind bluff. He is trusting that you know what lies ahead and what you are doing. The rider is trusting that the horse will not falter and keep his footing. Between the two of you, you will both arrive at the bottom safe.

God asks us to do the same. To place our trust in Him fully, in turn Jesus will care for us. To obey His commandments completely, and we will spend eternity in heaven together.

Tied Hard

An old cowboy never takes for granted, the tools of the trade. Everything must be in top condition, the saddle, the rigging, the rope. They don't have to be pretty, but like the horse they must have been tried and tested in all extremes. There have been found a trust and soundness in them all. He knows when he gathers or overtakes the herd there's bound to be one ol heifer that will break and run, in that moment the old cowboy is prepared. He has placed all confidence in his horse and tack. The rope is tied hard, he knows the speed is there to overcome, and the power is there to take the trip. He throws the loop, pitches the slack, rides by and steps off. When the dust clears, the old cowboy knows he will be standing on the ground, that ol heifer tied at his feet, he will look up and find his horse sound, the saddle and rigging in tact and a stretched rope. All was accomplished because he had prepared himself well, tied hard and trusted in his horse. You see, he could have used his horse the way we sometimes use God. He could have expected the horse to accomplish all by himself, without the asking. He could have asked and not accepted the power, or maybe just not tying hard, just holding the rope in his hand. He could have not checked the rigging and had a cinch or latigo that would not hold. The sad truth of the matter is he will not accomplish or he'll end up in a big ol wreck. It's the same with us, we just never get started or we find ourselves in a big ol wreck, Satan on top.

A Cowboy's Thoughts

Boots

Merle Roehr

If These Boots Could Talk

If these boots could talk,
of the long walk they've walked.
Oh what a story they might tell.

They're the first thing on.
They're the last thing off.
They've been with us quite a spell.

But if they talked,
of all their walk.
Oh I'm sure they'd be tales we'd need to quell.

They'd sometimes give us quite a rush.
They'd sometimes even make us blush.
But sure as sin they'd ring our bell.

Sometimes we do a lot of talking.
Sometimes we do a lot of walking.
Seems we're always trying to make a sell.

A Cowboy's Thoughts

But all in all we think we're safe.
Old boots can't talk, so we save face.
So from man we'll be spelled
he's not seen us as we fell.

But from ol God, we can't hide.
And on all these things He'll decide.
So it's on God's judgement all will tell.

Merle Roehr

Riding the Line

A nuzzle by the beast,
is a wonder of trust.
And the swath of the curry
will remove the rough crust.
A foot in the stirrup
is not there by chance.
A seat in the saddle
is but to be blessed.
There's no better place
to be in our life,
than straight in the saddle
and right with our Christ.
To go through our life
with Him on our mind,
should be to have life
that seems short of time.
He gives us enjoyments
to have here on earth.
Mine's to mount
upon a deep girth.
Now the pleasure's all mine,

when with Christ I ride.
It's not always easy
to reach the sublime,
but reward will be great,
when with Him, I dine.

Merle Roehr

Jesus Wasn't A Cowman

There's not much we will not do
to bring joy to our life.
But seldom we would bring,
joy into others' strife.
Now there was a man who gave it all
for unmeasurable joy in mankind's life.

I've a hard time seeing Him as a cowman,
but He didn't profess as much.
It's said He came as a lowly shepherd,
and I'm glad that He did such.

You see a cowman,
would have been much too hard.
He has learned to push and shove
sometimes uncaring, hard as nails.

But even this cowmans looking still,
In his life for joy to fill.
all to often to his dismay
and his many appeals.

A Cowboy's Thoughts

Now this Jesus,
came for the cowman too.
A shepherd
as odd as it would seem.

I'm glad He came in such a way.
For as a cowman pushes
I'd have been pushed astray.
But as The Shepherd leads
I've learned to pay heed.

Now it's for this guidance that I pray,
and I'm left in hope,
for Jesus leads me all the way.

Anything, anyone,
any decisions that are made
around me,
affect my future.

If they don't
I am among the
most selfish person
in the world.

Merle Roehr

Love

Love is love only when it is given by the recipient of love.
A tattered tapestry is proof of love by the workmanship,
of the one who has given it,
And by the use of the one receiving it.

In Psalms 139 it speaks about
being fearfully and wonderfully made.

And about weaving together with an inner core.
That inner core is love,
might it be in a quilt or a weaving
or any simple heirloom.

It is quite the same in our lives.
And the love that is given us by God is that inner core.

Love is only love when it is given by the recipient of love.

I want all to understand that poems are not always true to fact. In this particular poem the love of Christ is not portrayed. It was written for a special occasion and fit rather well, but would want all to know in Christ we should be able to give love unconditionally just as He gives us.

Merle Roehr

The Doubting Cowhand

An old cowhand sat at the back of a camp meeting. The circuit preacher talked of faith and action in God. Later the two talked into the night on the subject. The cowhand believing he had all that he needed, and the preacher being able to offer little in persuasions, was unable to move him. The cowhand had seen the wonders of God's creation and believed in God's control and believed he had let God have his life. The two set out late on their travels on separate trails. The cowhand not knowing his way around did not know the lay of the land. Somewhere in the late night and in his sleepiness the cowhand started to ponder the things the preacher had said. It was about that time the horse stumbled and threw the man over the edge of an unknown bluff. The cowhand slid and scrambled until he finally grasps hold of a stout juniper limb, the rest of him hanging in open air, unable to look down. He spent a great deal of the rest of the night crying for God's help. He just knew, that two or three times he had heard answers. The words kept coming "turn loose, I'll catch you," The trust just wasn't there. The old cowhand continued to hold on in strength and determination, he just wouldn't give up on himself. When the light began to come across the sky, the old preacher, having been in the river bed all night encouraging the cowhand, began to see the situation. The cowhand was just a few feet out of his reach. He once again told the cowhand to trust him and let go, he was just a few feet from him, he would catch him. The cowhand's response was simply "I just can't I've held on too long"

We are a little like that cowhand a lot of the time. We depend on our own power so long, we just can't turn loose.

If you would read from your Bible Eph. 3:13-19, it would do each of us well to release our grip on our power and start to realize the power of our God. This comes through study and real faith, action in belief.

Large troubles are but small,
when we are with God.

My intent in life is
to form some type of
relationship with every person I meet.
I may not succeed in all cases,
due to their attitude
or more especially mine.
But if I don't have intent
nothing will ever happen.

Merle Roehr

Prayer Among the Heifers

In a great deal of my story telling and poetry, I use the phrase or thought (to call upon the Lord). In this aspect of life, I was taught that prayer was as continual as my life, that it was in every part of living. I hope this story will relate the necessity of prayer. The fact that no matter how large or small the problem is, God is always there and never to busy to listen. The story is nothing extra but it brought me a long way in life as just a simple reminder. In that this situation was important enough for Him to help with, it is a reminder, He is there always.

As it was, I had taken the job on the ranch late in the summer of that year. There was one other hand and he was in much need, at the time. He was watering cane and the time was upon us to sow wheat. A great deal of the work that I was hired to do is and was not considered ranch work by many. The work however was a necessity and cattle need feed. Now most of us know that there is more to running a ranch than being a cowboy. There was a time when ranches were grand and there are still a few. Within those ranches there was the possibility of specialized jobs. Nevertheless,

A Cowboy's Thoughts

I had a vast job description, and I was all the more blessed with the abilities to do the various works.

I had replaced a man and later another who had proclaimed themselves as great cowboys. Now I would not judge their character nor their ability, but in these times you must be able to do more than just sit on top of a horse or push a cow. Modern ranch work says you have to be a cowman. The two terms do not have anything to do with maturity but with responsibility within the organization. As I said, my responsibilities were vast. When I was moved in and settled, the boss man showed me around, there was, as I said, the farming to help with. There were also the branding and weaning to deal with which involved about twenty two-hundred head of mama cows. In among all of this I had counted forty-two windmills to be brought up to par, half had not operated in over a year. There seemed to be an unsurmountable amount of work, but things seemed to go quite smooth through the fall and early winter. We accomplished the cow work and had put up most of the feed, the wheat was growing well, most of the mills were running and those that weren't would not be much trouble.

There was, however, one thing that was very much on my mind. There was the calving of the heifers in the spring, I had been told they would start sometime in May. Oh, I had calved heifers, but not on this scale. I had also noticed that there were a few that were already piggy (a term used to describe, heavy with a calf) in January. I was told it should be a short season, but the first thing I had done in August was to pull the Red Brangus bulls out of the heifer pastures. I had also culled the cross and scrub (stock considered substandard) heifers. I needed to be able to see over what was there. It seemed the man before, had kept more than two hundred head, just a few too many for our purpose. By the time we had finished there was around one hundred ten head. They were in three different pastures on four sections of land. I was not seeing this as a pleasurable task, for all the things there were to do, the heifers were far too scattered. I did not know that the worst was yet to come. The heifers were all strong, healthy, and heavy, they for the most part were on good wheat pasture, and were Herefords. All that I knew and had been taught, made this a good situation. It did however look like this season was about to start early and I knew it would end late. The first of March came and along and with it came deep snow and the first calf. The fun was upon us. Now the calf came easy and healthy, but it was mighty cold and new mamas are not always good mamas. I then started to realize that to take a heifer and calf anywhere, it was over a mile and three narrow gates. It seemed I had no choice. I picked up the calf then fought that heifer through those gates to a place a calf could survive. The problems still weren't too bad, it just took a little time and work, both which were available. All the early calves came easy, but all too soon things would change. Seems one day in May, one ol heifer was having tremendous problems. I had assumed that the calf was coming backwards. Now a cow in pain, which has been there for a considerable time is not too controllable. Their mind seems only to be on the fight. When we finally found the barn and put that heifer in the chute, the calf was right, but seemed terribly big. I did some checking on the bulls and found that with the Red Brangus bulls, calves would weigh around fifty pounds, but this calf was big. At this time I attributed the size to the heifer's background or that she had crossed the fence, accidents happen. A big problem, the situation became the norm. I had been really good at calving, but most of this was becoming disheartening for someone who thought things had to be perfect or at least realistic.

There were a couple of things I didn't know about the last hand that was there. I never did know if there had been some shady events or just dissatisfactions. There did seem however to be some vengeful happenings. After I had visited with the neighbors, I found this to be evident. Now there were no other hands that knew about the happenings around this camp, not even the boss man. After the man had been given walking papers, he told of turning the Santa Gertrudis bulls in with the heifers. Now those of us who know cattle, know that this is not a good thought, but it happened and I had to deal with it. The boss man gave me his condolences but there was still a job to do. The cross is mighty good when you have big cows, but these were young heifers. This presented big problems. I was calving heifers with calves at a hundred pounds or more. In the time of calving I lost fourteen head of heifers and twenty-five head of calves. In the middle part of June the situation reverted back. I all of the sudden had small calves again. As you will recall, I had pulled Brangus bulls out of the pastures when I took the job. Now I never did know if the man hated the boss man, or just did not know any better, but he spent a lot of time moving bulls. Between that and the weight of the Santa Gertrudis bulls, accounted for the length of the calving season, it seems it took five months to calf heifers.

Now God works with each of us in different ways, but He works with us where we are and I was on the ranch, on a horse most of the time. Now that's where He found me. I needed very much so to depend on God more, I believe this was the start. Now in this situation God will not change what man has built. There were many times I would sit on that back porch and pray for smaller calves, and in a way I received smaller calves late in the season. This was due to another mans changing the bulls after the hand was fired, without knowing what he had done. I believe this was God's plan for me, if I used it. Now we seem to always ask for big help for big problems. Somewhere in the middle of calving season, on top of a big red horse I started asking for small things. As I said, I had heifers scattered all over the place, with many fences and gates between them, and the refuge of calving. I was not a roper, nor was I experienced in the art of cowboying as much as the want to be one. I sat on that horse many a morning, asking for that rope to land where it belonged or for that heifer to slip through that eight-foot gate in the middle of a mile long fence. If you have ever seen stock in pain, control does not come easy. In this time I watched heifers slip through one to three of those eight foot gates and never slow down. There are many things that teach us each day. Most times they seem small and insignificant. Now all in all it sounds odd, but I have often wondered of those days. Now don't get me wrong I know that God did not appear physically but, He has told us that if we are seeking Him, He will be with us. Now at the time, those heifers going through those gates, never bobbled. I have often mused that God could have been saddled up hazing those ol heifers through. See we can't do things on our own, prayer is needed and no need is too small. It's something we all need to remember and grasps hold of.

What did a Mother See?

I ponder the thoughts of Mary.
Were they thoughts of pain and fears?
Were her thoughts of joy within the tears?

I would believe from the heart came tears to weep.
Did they come from knowing, His life was complete?
Did they come from Him laying, His life at God's feet?

I ponder, did it tear her heart in two
to see Him at their hand's abuse?
I ponder, did she see the joy
did she understand God's use?

I ponder, did she look at the past
and see the use of His life at last?
As she looked at Him there on the cross,
could she see love and hate, in the life that He had lost?

The emotions must have been vast,
as she watched Him breath his last.

Merle Roehr

> I ponder, her thoughts when told, He was risen.
> Of all the hope He had given.
>
> Can I take the time to ponder, thoughts
> not hers', but mine?
> Will I realize the wonders He has wrought,
> all the souls He has bought?
>
> Can I cry the tears that His mother cried?
> Because of this, I can with Him abide.

A Christmas Thought

I'm spose to be feedin cattle,
but it's a rough ol road to go.
Seems it been covered over,
with a beautiful stuff called snow.

So I sit here on edge of that ol cap-rock,
and watch it dustin one of them natural frocks.

I'm sure there's been many a cowboy here,
Just to think on a bit o Christmas cheer.
And even with all the white stuff fallin,
it seems to be mighty clear.

Now I don't know when,
our Good Lord was born.
And it don't matter much.
What I see as a more portant task,
is the two of us stay in touch.

Now it might be strange to see me visit,
when they ain't but one of us here.

And if you look a might closer,
you'll see two pretty clear.

Seems a lot of people practice the season,
and go their merry way.
Now Christ was born and died for me
in that land afar away.
And when He arose from that ol grave,
I was asked to live it every day.
Now I'll put that old Bible back in my ol truck,
and go about my task.
And He'll lead me out the other side,
and I'll in His Glory bask.

God has given in abundance,
let us accept it graciously.

My Anchor

I use many ideas, most derived from ranching. This one came from my Dad, but it's roots are still in ranching. A great deal of my growing up years my dad was teaching me the art of building fence. One term he always used was "deadman." I always wanted to know who we were going to put in the hole, it took me years to understand what was going on. For those who would not understand the term, it was the anchor at the end of the line of a fence. We all see the corner posts and understand they are there, but there still has to be an anchor. It is part of the corner but my dad always buried it deep, it was never seen.

Just because we don't see an anchor does not mean it is not there, remember the fence is still standing. We must understand that Christ had to die, be buried, and resurrected. He is my way to the Father. God is my anchor. I must stand within the fence.

Merle Roehr

Anchored

Anchored

I am a tree, small and sturdy.
Not able to stand on my own.
I stand here only under the power of an anchor.
I am anchored deep in the rock. There is my strength.

I could be the Christian, small and sturdy.
Not able to stand on my own.
I stand here only under the power of an anchor.
I am anchored deep in the rock. God is my strength.

All the memories in the world
won't build the future.

You never know
what the future holds,
until you look back
and watch the past unfold.

Merle Roehr

Nothing so Delightful as Peach Cobbler and Apricot Jam

No matter where you find a ranch cook, no matter who they may be, the worn out cowhand, the short fat cook, or the lady at headquarters. The chucks gotta be good, the coffee has always gotta be hot, and stew is always thick with big chunks of meat. There might be times when things are a little thin and beans and salt pork will have to do, but there is always a pot cooking and you never go hungry and the grub is never bad. There might be beef hanging in the windmill tower or fresh killed venison. Steak and tatters are always fine and dandy. A breakfast of eggs and biscuits or pancakes and syrup are always handy. But a cowhand knows nothing can calm the soul like a spoon of peach cobbler or the taste of apricot jam.

There are many ways
to cook a cat.
It is deciding to eat it
that becomes the problem.

Recipes
Loin Stuff

6 to 8 inches of loin trimmed clean of all excess fat, and the silver membrane as much as possible. Slice through one side of the loin, to make as large a pocket as possible without making any part to thin. Stuff with grated cheese. There are many options, from here. One item may be enough, but there can be many combinations. Any type cheese: Cheddar - Swiss - Muenster.

Any kind of nut: Pinon - Pecan - Almond - Walnut. Spices or aromatics: Garlic - Pepper - Onion - Thyme. Peppers: Chiles - Jalapenos -Scotch Bonnets. Even crumbled bacon or diced, fried fatback The combinations are unlimited, choose the flavors that seem to fit your taste, or those that compliment. I use strong flavored cheeses with strong meats. Example with venison I use a sharp aged cheddar with garlic and onion. Mix enough cheese and spices to fill the pocket in the loin, then close with a large needle and cotton string or weave a bamboo skewer through the slit in the meat to close. Seer all sides in cast iron skillet with just enough peanut or olive oil. When brown, place in oven at

300 and cook to desired doneness, remove and let set five to ten minutes then slice with sharp knife.

Walnut Compost

1 cup fine diced walnuts
1 cup diced dried apricots
1/4 cup butter
8 to 16 oz. cream cheese
equal or sugar to taste
whole nutmeg

Sweat walnuts in butter in a skillet just enough to change texture and roasted flavor then let cool so as not to melt cream cheese when added. Mix apricots and walnuts then add to cream cheese. When mixed well, add sweetener until it suits your taste, then grate nutmeg, small amounts at a time. You want just enough nutmeg to taste. I usually put this mixture on crepes, 2 tbsp. should be enough, then roll and cool. Serve them cool with a fruit, cream, or fruit sauce over or under them. The compost can be served on crackers, but would be better with more cream cheese in the mix. The mix has as many options as you have ideas, just mix and match with the theme of your meal. Here are just a few ideas: raisins, cardamon, ginger - apples, cinnamon - peaches, cardamon, nutmeg.

Merle Roehr

Crepes

2 tbsp. melted butter
1 ½ cups milk
2/3 cup flour
½ tsp. salt
3 eggs

Mix all these ingredients in mixing bowl until smooth. Cover and refrigerate for two hours. Coat a six to eight-inch nonstick skillet with thin coat butter over medium heat. Pour in 1/4 cup of batter, much the same as pancakes, but cover whole pan very thin. Cook about two minuets then lift edge with a metal spatula and loosen, turn over for thirty seconds then place on wax paper. You may later stack them with wax paper between. Place in a container those that are extra and freeze.

Strawberry Christmas Sauce

3 lbs. frozen strawberries
if using fresh you will need water
½ cup cranberries, fresh
pinch of ground cardamon
pinch of grated nutmeg
two or three juniper berries crushed fine
sugar or Splenda to taste
one or two tsp. orange zests, fresh is a must
corn starch or arrowroot to thicken to desired thickness

This can be used as a syrup, jam or sauce, on toast, nut breads, pancakes and the likes. It is even great with ice creams, toppings and various other ideas. Only the lack of imagination limits you.

Stew the strawberries, using only as much water as necessary, add cranberries and cook down. When cooked down to the consistency you wish then add sugar, spices and orange zest. The sugar will thin a little. The taste can be tart to syrup, you decide. If it is not at the desired thickness, the corn starch or the arrowroot will thicken. The arrowroot will give a more glossy appearance. The sauce is very tasteful and aromatic.

Cowboy Coffee

Cowboy coffee, a coffee of choice.
For the one who chooses, chooses a life.
One that for most is hard and unfit,
same as the coffee they drink.
Dark, hard and straight from the fire
it often looks as a bucket of mire.
In ways the coffee portrays a life.
One, some consider full of strife,
rough and gravely is this chewable mix.
Sometimes as pointed as good mesquite stix.
But the elixir is as sweet to the cowboy
as honeysuckle to the bees voyage.
It wakes him up, it warms him up,
it relaxes at the end of day.
It seems the cowboy's life is built on this stew.
Friendships are renewed and made over the brew.
We call it coffee.
So if you wish to be one,
pull up a rock and pour one

Merle Roehr

You know you're past your prime when,
the most common aroma that reaches your senses
is that of mint.

The Good Cup o Coffee

It's hard to find a cup o coffee now days.
One that I'd consider good somehow.
Many a places now advertise,
your drink of choice and how!
And all the drinks you'll find there in
will make you feel the wow!

There are flavors a-many,
and sights a-plenty.
With all the gadgets
these luscious delights can sell.

I find bold flavor can be brewed
in that old coffee pot yet.
And you can know it's the best coffee
your ever gonna get.
From a bed of coals or the ol wood stove,
the taste will ne'er be met.

For all the flavor or
sights you'll find.

Merle Roehr

> An ol tin cup and black metal pot
> are all the tac you'll pine.
> And then the sight of the ol campfire
> will be the most sublime.

Things I've Learned # 2

This idea was brought about,
by the thought of another man.
I decided to take the thought and modify it to
my way of understanding.

Impression upon my being,
without the chance of expression from within,
only leaves me with depression.

If you get the curb strap
to tight on the horses bits,
you get rebellion instead of control,
you can do the same with children.

Sometimes it takes
a whole lot of reality,
to know what is real.
I had to stand behind the mule,
before I knew he'd kick with both hind feet.

Life is a whole lot like riding a bronc.
If you don't relax before you hit the ground,
your going to hurt mightily.
If you don't get up and get back on,
he's going to win.

Coffee is a subject on which many have ideas.
I am an avid coffee drinker,
often it's mighty strong
and there are those who complain of my brew.
I was also brought up with this thought.
There's no such thing as strong coffee,
Just weak people.
I hate hot, colored water!

I grew up listening to my Dad tell of an episode in his younger days of growing up. He and a friend, who grew up with him on a ranch in the Texas panhandle, decided to have some good old fashioned fun. The two of them took a couple of the local ol tom cats, tied their tails together and hung them over the clothes line. Well my father was cared for by a black women at times, when she discovered the situation, her discipline was for the two boys to remove the cats from the line and untie them. Now I would not know from experience, but am told they received quite a revelation. There maybe only one thing more difficult than tying two tom cat's tails together, and that would be getting the two apart. From my way of thinking, it would be a good idea to consider the final results,before committing yourself to any snap decision.

Jessie

Joy is like the little girl who takes a bite of lemon,
and grins from ear to ear, from the feeling in her mouth.
It is that which comes from inside her, that brings pleasure,
not what is happening around her.
So it is, with the joy we have in Christ,
it is that which is within that brings pleasure,
not those things of the world that might happen around us.

In our raising many children, It seems that we are always encouraging one or two of them to catch up. Now there are always those who continue to lag behind. As adults all we can do is lead by example and encourage. I have never been able to make one of them do what they did not wish to.

Somewhere in life they will either, catch up or become lost.

God is somewhat the same, He encourages us with His example and gift, but we must decide what we will do. He does not wish for any to be left behind, but He will not make any do His will. It is our decision to catch up or be lost.

Children's Memories

I believe that most of us would agree that children's lives should be full of good memories. The great problem is, they are not. There are some of us who are blessed to share our lives with children. To date there has been sixty of them, live within my home and countless others, we have been involved with. When we started in child care, I had a thought that I believe we should all consider.

Other than a belief in God, the most important thing I can give a child is that of good and joyous memories. My job is that of giving good memories. I hope I accomplish that feat. I feel at times I fall short in that effort. Maybe this, is what drives me.

Of all the complaining that's done in life
about what we're given, I have had a thought.
If you look a gift horse in the mouth long enough,
He's bound to jump up and bite you.

High Standards

My father and granddad, were both big men in my mind. My father was so tall and my grandad was so broad. My dream had always been to be like them. I was always dragging a catch rope or wearing a pair of spurs or a hat that was two sizes too big and never wore anything but boots. They made you big too. It's hard to imagine, but somewhere in my thirties, I realized I was both taller than my dad and broader than my grandad. I am now over forty and still looking up. I still see myself dragging a catch rope or wearing a pair of spurs. The hat I wear fits now, and yes I still wear boots. I have realized that these men are not as big physically, but sometimes I still feel like a little boy. For I now understand, that the true measure of men is not measured by stature, but are measured from within.

Merle Roehr

The Rescue

I saw him sitting in that old cedar brush.
It seemed as though his world was crushed.

Although the sun was bright and bold.
The little boy's face was gray and cold.

You could tell the little boy was there in hurt.
By all the tears there in the dirt

I approach him just as quiet as I can.
He's like a pup, been kicked around.
I talk to him softly as an ol cowboy can,
but from his lips came not a sound.

I've never had much, but they were always there.
To give me comfort anytime anywhere.

I have nothing to give cept my horse and my dog.
But they're his to have for only a nod.

A Cowboy's Thoughts

I gently lift him over my head.
I set him up there on top of old Red.

There in the saddle, with his first big ol smile.
I believe you could see it for over a mile

I never knew of his maw or his paw.
They never did show, for even a call.

He spent growing days with me and my wife.
Although some days were spent full of strife
And when he's grown up, there'll be secrets come out.
He had just been deserted, there was never a doubt.

There may be some things you never will hear.
But remember the cause is only from his fear.

But there'll be one day the thanks will be yours
If all has been given sincerely and pure.

People will never come close,
if we are always pushing them back.

Merle Roehr

The Little Girl's Flowers

She picked a flower,
t'wasn't much.
We adults all pitched
us quite a fuss.

We want to be good parents,
but all too often just play a part.
So I placed it in my old hat band,
to save her precious heart.

We fume and fuss and make
those small unheard of rules.
So when we find them broken,
we often blow a fuse.
Now little children in innocence,
they haven't got a clue.

They do it all with precious souls,
their only there to please.
We often miss their simple pleasures
cause we refuse to see.

A Cowboy's Thoughts

So we as parents, go through life,
much confused with all our thoughts.
Because we trade the innocence,
for unwritten rules we've wrought.

So when we
stop playing a part.
Take a flower,
save a child's precious heart.

Merle Roehr

The Lady

I met a lady today, small and quite
with a bursting vibrant hue.
I have always called her a lady,
for she was always true.
It ran much, much deeper than this,
for all the qualities came through.
And all of those who knew her all along the way,
are now her children too.
It seems her time is finished here,
we remembered her today.
Now we must know her memories
will push the hurt away.
I used to think of ladies
only in their youth.
It's possible my thoughts
have often been confused.
You see this lady,
was all of ninety-two.

It is possible that we see things in different shades, partly because of age, maturity and the happenings that occur around us. I have been privileged to know (how shall I say this) some very mature women, who had much wisdom to impart, in very few words. I hope I have been able to hang onto it. Their age and experience had developed wonderful, lovely ladies. Oh, they were women, but the qualities of a lady were so strong that you were impressed at first sight. Up till death they did not cease to have that impression on me.

Merle Roehr

Daughters

I believe we never know how special daughters are to their fathers. It's not until they become young ladies and launch out on their own that we realize their importance to us. I am faced with this at this time, as mine steps out at the age of seventeen to go overseas. It is at a time of great disruption (5/24/02). She is going to teach God's Word to others.

Sometime yesterday, I looked back, and she was but a baby. She was someone with character to build. Her mother and I asked God to help us guide her. She grew up in a world like most, but she was serious, industrious, independent, and most of all special. She grew as a young girl does, always full of life, always considering others in their ways. To me she was building her personality on what she saw as good in others. She continued to love life, she worked hard in all things, I think she saw them as a foundation in her life.

As she grew into a young lady, she strove to look to God. She grew sturdy and independent of man, but dependent on God. I am not saying that she does not have the problems of a young lady, she does. Sometimes she handles them

A Cowboy's Thoughts

right and sometimes wrong, but I believe she seeks God's answers.

Yesterday, I looked toward tomorrow, and I saw a young woman. One with character, but most of all one with faith in God. I am so glad we asked for His help. It hurts so to see her separate herself from me, but the work chosen is important. I am now once again asking God to help me let her go. He has helped us build her on our request. She is now His, so the best I can do is ask that He will go with her, and let her live a full life, and while she does, keep her and her soul safe.

The only piece of advice I can give to parents is to pray for that little girl before she is born, ask God to help build her, and expect success then give her to God.

Merle Roehr

Sons

I have a son, one in whom I place a great deal of pride in and respect for. At age fourteen, he is willing to do and carry himself well, while doing it. He is sometimes terribly arrogant, but at fourteen it's as should be, one day it will be a good tool under control. He is often as brave as anyone I have known, he has already faced more problems than most, and been able to overcome with God's help. Along with these qualities he seems to be humble, and with the kindest heart I have ever seen. I picture him finding that of being a great man, one who achieves it from the inside. He is not complete by any means, there is still need for more maturing, as is for me. For those who are just starting out in raising a son, there is a great deal of work and hard times ahead. I have just one piece of advice, seek the help of God. The road is long and hard to becoming a man, but with God the blessings are rich.

A Cowboy's Thoughts

The Dog

Merle Roehr

The Survival of The Everlasting Prairie Dog
A study by the cowboy

It might be important for me to first give to you my qualifications. I have lived among the prairie dogs *(*genus *Cynomys,* esp. *C. ludovicianus* of the prairie*)* a burrowing rodent, which has existed even before colonial America, since I was a small boy. I first was a tormentor of this small creature and had a great fondness for destroying their burrows. I later graduated to the art of long distant shooting sports and considered them wonderful targets. I lived on ranches where they were prevalent and over populated. I acquired the ability to dislike their presence. I was, however, disappointed in my lack of ability to remove them from the premises on which I lived, although we tried. I now live with just a small populated town of these creatures that are considered a health threat to anything that passes among them. I have still not been able to find a solution to the problem of eradication. Thus, I have put together a short study of their habits and stamina.

A Cowboy's Thoughts

There may be two definitions that we need to know as we study the prairie dog. The first is survival. The continuation of life or to outlive all other things, in this instance it is carrying on beyond all creatures. The second is the prairie dog, which in further reference will be simply called, dog. The dog as we said earlier is a burrowing rodent, it seems to be ever present on our prairies, especially from the middle to the western United States, and from some parts of Canada to the farther parts of South America.

By the animal rights lobbyist, it is considered a loveable irresistible creature. That which should be able to roam freely over every part of the country, to penetrate and aerate our land at all cost. To others, the total annihilation of the furry little beast would be recommended and greatly appreciated. I do not believe that either of these groups has an inclination of what they might be asking. To follow the ideas of one group would mean to remove all vegetation from the sod we live upon. The other would remove the presence of the comical little creatures, and its source of great enjoyment for the coyote *(Canis latrans)*, another creature which finds much dispute in North America. It would also bring great harm to a creature known as the prairie rattler (family Crotalidae, genera *Sistrurus* and *Crotalus)*, a very well known and appreciated family of reptiles.

Now it is in my opinion after great study, if we are to let this rodent, the dog, exist as it pleases and remove all harm from it, we would be in great danger of extinction. The dog would also cease to exist, but then who would care. There is a need for some type of balance in their existence. It seems that through study, although this is not an exact science only because of the difference in climate and general location, the dog would cleanse the earth of vegetation. It is known that the dog will eat everything, anywhere from six feet to sixty feet according to the amount of vegetation that is sustained within that area. Whatever the distance might be, double that and it becomes the distance between holes. We have seen that when the vegetation has been depleted, the dogs will migrate the distance that is necessary to survive. The moving of the dogs, in turn gives much room for beetles, snakes and various other vermin to take over. This is a never-ending cycle.

To drive them into extinction, seems would be an almost impossible task. When I lived on the ranch, the state demanded us to rid the land of the dog. There were various methods. Most had to do with terminating them. There were however other methods, one was to drown them out, take them captive, thus selling the fur-balls as pets. A great plus for both groups, seeing that they were kept alive, and the ranchers made a small amount of money. I have only seen this in a case or two and it seemed to work very well. There were however a couple of drawbacks in the idea. It was decided by a select few, that the dog might carry rabies maybe, maybe not. I never was made privy to any of their test. The other was if you owned the dog as a pet you were at risk of being inflicted with great injury. It seems those four front teeth had the precision sharpness of a surgeon's scalpel, and they didn't mind using them. The other method of removing the dog, was to use a huge vacuum mounted on a truck and relocate them to new habitats. That habitat soon became over populated and barren.

Now that we have examined both sides of the issue, I must state my stand. I have been on both sides of the argument at times. I have first been placed over the task of eradication of the dog as vermin, an immeasurable task and one that was not so pleasurable. It seems there was always a hot blistering sun or a blustering wind with a great deal

A Cowboy's Thoughts

of dust and dirt. This is not to make mention of the hiding rattlers. On the other hand I am a lover of nature and believe everything has a place. I do see a place of great value for the dog. There are always those photographic opportunities with their comical antics. There is short and long range rifle practice and even the chance to hone one's shotgunning abilities. There is the necessity to fill the rattler's belly and keeping the coyotes full, thus protecting the calving situation in the spring. For the more exotic living, there is always the potential possibility of a good hearty, healthy, organic grown stew after the dog has fattened on that expensive grown grass. All in all, they have their place.

Now to get on with their abilities to survive. As I have said, this is theory and not an exact science, but the other side uses the same criteria in their proof. I have spent most of my life observing this small creature, maybe closer than others through the clarity of a good scope, a 4X32 where they are brought into close viewing range. They seem to be intense, private creatures especially under fire, so most of their time is spent underground. I have decided that their breeding rites take place underground in late summer or fall. This is in contradiction of others' suggestions of late winter to spring. These things I have never actually witnessed, but we do usually depopulate a dog town the late fall. This also brings another theory. It is in the late fall we kill out a town and in the early spring the small immature dogs begin to run rampant. I have theorized that they are one of two mammals that lay eggs. The other is the platypus *(Ornithorhynchus anatinus)* if one mammal can lay eggs why not another. There is however the necessity of moisture to hatch eggs. This is also quite easily explained. These burrows are so deep and vast that there is either a storage for water or they are dug to the water table. This seems to explain the reason for their ability of not needing surface water and for the exceptional hatch ability of their eggs. I do not yet understand the process of the hatching of the dog's eggs. Nor do we know the temperature to hold the eggs through the winter months or at the time of hatching. In normal circumstances the ground temperature at that depth should hold at around sixty degrees Fahrenheit, but I have no way of ascertaining that information at this time. I have however concluded that a clutch consists of from seven to fifteen eggs, thus explaining the population explosion of a dog town in early spring that has previously been killed out. It also indicates that the adult of the species is not necessarily needed to help raise the young.

In my studies I have come to the conclusion that it would be an impossibility to exterminate the entire population of dogs. I have spent many years on one place trying and every year they seemed to be more plentiful than the year before. As I have said before this is just in theory, but so are all other studies on the idea. And in science, is it not the theory that all studies are based on.

Be generous with
your opinions.
Keep them to yourself.

A Cowboy's Thoughts

Up for Chuck

Sometime early in the nineteen hundreds, when cow work was becoming a big industry here in the United states, there was a humorous story told of early rising. It was from the chuck wagon that it was being told. Now as it was on most ranches the days started early and ended late. It was not like today, even though we think we work mighty long, hard hours, we can't even come close.

Well it seems that an old cowboy, tired of those early morns or a young man not being to work brittle, had grown weary. The cook was always responsible for rousting the cowhands from their bedrolls before breakfast. The cowhands in turn readied the tack and the horses for the day's work. They had done such and had found their first cup of coffee. The morn was still dark and enough clouds to hide most of the stars, the old cook suggested that the boys start breakfast, in order to complete the task before sunrise, and so it was. Seems the boys had plenty of time. They decided to drink another cup of coffee. Well one cup lead to another, and it was as if the morn drug on for an eternity.

Seeing as if there was plenty of time, this ol cowhand had a grand suggestion. His thought was as such "If'in we're

Merle Roehr

gonna set here all mornin, we just as well start dinner." Seems the cook let them do just that. Dinner finished the cook cleaned up, the hands drinking coffee and waiting for daylight. Each continued readying themselves for the day. The morn was dark and cool, and light just wasn't coming over the hill. The ol cowhand seeming just a little disgruntled came up with another suggestion "there's no use in wastin good time let's just eat supper too." The Old cook just went ahead and served the evening meal too. The hands ate their fill and lounged around the fire and enjoyed their coffee. The ol cowhand lumbered off and unsaddled his horse, kicked out his bedroll and sat down and started to pull his boots. The sun was just starting over the ridge. The old cook then questioned his actions pretty sternly, with that the old cowhand retorted back with "Where'en I comes from we retires after our supper." With that said, he crawled in his roll.

Now as you know this is a rather exaggerated little story. Yet I know that morns on the wagon start mighty early and the days were mighty long. So remember when you think your morning is early and your day is long, we can always go back to the good old days.

A Cowboy's Thoughts

This story was told me as a little boy by my granddad, Chester Arthur Roehr. When I was a boy, we would visit my grandparents. They lived on a ranch that had been owned by several companies. It was originally owned by the JA's to the best of my knowledge, they called the place Spring Creek. The house was in the lower part of the canyons just above the river. Between the house and the river it was mostly tall grass and brush, with about ten of the biggest old cottonwoods I have ever seen, up close to the house. There was not a television or even electricity at the house. There seemed to be nothing to spoil the family enjoyment. The house had a large front porch where we spent a great deal of our evenings watching turkeys going to roost and listening to his stories. This one I remember most interesting, puzzling, and was most remembered. It was always my favorite. Being that I was a boy, and one who believed everything his granddad said to be the truth, this is the story he told.

Eaten by Wolves

I had decided one cold and snowy morning to run my trap lines and to hunt for a little meat. I set out early morning and began to work the trap lines. It was sometime after good daylight I spied a nice young buck standing in a small clump of brush. He looked just right to hang in the meat house, for the winter eating. I eased along slowly so as not to spook him until I was close enough for a good sure shot. It had been an easy shot, so I set about to dress him out and get him ready to pack out after I had run the rest of the trap line. Sometime after the noon meal I had finished the traps and started for the deer. As I walked through the rough brush I felt a strange presence but I decided to continue, it seems I had never had anything to have a fear of in these parts before. I found the deer about three in the afternoon. I spent a short time to take on a little nourishment before continuing on my way. The time would be well after dark when I arrived at the line camp. There was still that strange feeling of the presence of something or someone looming over me. After I finished and started off toward home, I entered into open country. It was after I had traveled about a half of a mile I started to relax. The relaxing was premature. In the next hundred yards or so I caught a glimpse of what appeared to be wolves. I decided that I must place a greater distance between me and them. The dressed carcass of the buck I was carrying, I threw to the ground feeling that the wolves would stop and eat it. This was with the assumptions that there were just a few. I thought that might give me the time to get home. Within a few hundred yards I noticed they had devoured the deer carcass. It seemed to look like there were at least twenty-five of them now, and they looked to be gaining ground on me. I took careful aim at the leader of the pack and downed him. Thinking that would scatter them, you can understand my astonishment when they gathered and consumed him. There was the thought that this would give me another chance, but as I traveled the snow became deeper and harder to travel. As I glanced back, I noticed them on my trail again. The particular incident of shooting the wolf that took the lead recurred every two or three hundred yards for the rest of the day. Without fail those wolves that were left consumed the one wolf that had been shot, and then continued on my trail. Toward dark I thought I had finally escaped the pack. I decided to stop to rest for a few moments, just then I heard what sounded like a low growl, over my shoulder there was the biggest, blackest wolf I had ever seen. I stopped and carefully aimed thinking I would have at least a hide to take home. He needed to be in as close as he would come, I wanted a good shot. When he looked close enough, I squeezed the trigger. All I heard was the hollow click of the hammer on an empty chamber. I had been so busy and worried trying to escape, that I had forgotten to reload the rifle. There had also been such a need to take a short shot, I had let him in to close, I never had a chance. The wolf attacked and devoured me, bones and all. Not a trace of me was ever found. I am here to tell you, that this is truth.

I believe this to be true, because my granddad told me so, and you?

Merle Roehr

I See God's Hand

There is a book that gives us God's work. There are those things we must know and do to enter heaven's gates. As a cowboy there is a book that God gives us, I am privileged to see it each day, we call it nature. Within that nature we see God's hand, His eternal power and divine nature. The Good Book calls it creation. I see a canvas in the sky and the clouds that paint wonderful and beautiful pictures, ever changing and powerful, from softness to harshness. There is a gentleness that can be given in shading, to the harshness of thundering storms or blizzards of cold, unforgiving wind and snow. There is the majestic authority that I see in looking up at the mountains, crowned in that first snow of fall. There is the beauty of the trees as they are robed in their new colors at the awesome changing of the seasons. I can see the gentleness in a newborn calf or a fresh hatched chick, the care given the new life and the joy of it all.

Riding through any type country, it seems to me a man has no choice except to see the All Mighty God in all that surrounds him. If he can't see it, he is pushing his horse too hard and treating his stock wrong, but worst of all, he is becoming hard and callused without concern for others or himself. A man needs to slow his pace, look around, learn of creation, learn of the Creator. See God in all, observe His majestic power.

Rom. 1 : 19 - 20

Merle Roehr

Blue Storm Clouds

Those ol blue storm clouds up over the plains,
they stall they wait to bring their good rains.

More often than not they fall mighty short,
but be pretty sure you'll hear em report.

They'll bellow and rumble they'll bring a wind blow,
and a fire in them clouds will set a night glow.

They loom they threaten they bring dread and fear,
but here once again it's almost clear.

Now e'er so often their course is changed,
and we're once again blessed with God's gracious rain.

Now times it's torrid and times it's soft,
and times it's there just hanging aloft.

But ne'er a drop is e'er a loss,
for there's grass, the tanks and an ol wooden trough.

We're always glad to see it here,
when God is willing to let it appear.

Merle Roehr

The Coming of the Wind

In the coming of the wind,
it brings it's blessings,
it brings it's tolls.

Oh the howls can bring
vibrant vivid thoughts to a mind.

I can listen, and at times
I can see it's terrible blustering cold.
Then there are times,
I see the dry hot breath
of some monstrous beast.

Those thunder heads
they boil, they rise high in the sky,
ready to strike their toil.
We know water is fixin to roll
and the wind's achin to blow.

I see the smoke of a fire
out on that prairie there.

A Cowboy's Thoughts

Being pushed , as a slave,
of an unseen awesome power.

Yet in all our terrible thoughts we see,
pleasantries there are to be.

The soft summer breeze
the calm thoughts we see.
The rattling of an old mill,
the flowing grass
the rustling of cottonwood trees.

Of all the sight we can hear,
they're brought on unseen wings of air.

We must see of all that coming,
brings a myriad of musings,
some good, some bad.

But all come from God's hands,
and their place we must see.
It might just be His way of saying
you should be with me.

We can hear it blow
we watch it flow.

We may even harness it's might,
but the one thing we'll never do,
is quell it's awesome right.

Merle Roehr

Ugly

I have in all my life lived in various places,
all different.
I have listened to folks talk
about how terrible or ugly
a place has been or is.
I have wondered
how one lives a life
of joy and happiness,
when they cannot see
the beauty of God's creation.
The only way to live
an enjoyable life
is to realize what God has given
and He is the giver.

A Cowboy's Thoughts

Beauty

Merle Roehr

Beauty of life, Missed

I live in that rare beauty,
I talk about.
Problem is
I don't take notice
as I walk about.

The beauty of life
therein all about,
the proof of the noise,
that's heard throughout.

Oh I see plenty of things
to whet my appetite.
But in most cases I see them
in black and white.

I often hear the beauty
but only muted it seems.
I don't even take notice
of what quiet noises mean.

A Cowboy's Thoughts

Our eyes and ears
are here for our pleasures.
We seldom take note
of all these grand treasures.

So let us see and let us hear.
It's ever so wonderful and ever so clear.

Merle Roehr

Changed but not Gone

There were days
when the prairies were broad and bold.
There was much therein
in which to behold.

I've been told
that buffalo and elk roamed here.
Yet on what
it's not quite clear.

It was used by the cowman,
as much as one could hold.
To take on more
was a move much to bold.

Now I've throwed a few loops
and busted some rump.
Seems there's not much to throw at
cept a few stumps.

A Cowboy's Thoughts

The stock here is few
and far in between.
And the grass is further
If'n you know what I mean.

The only good grass
we see very near.
Is what them good city folks
take water to rear.

A great many o these things
are really still here.
But you must search
those hills far and near.

Oh for sure there are things here to be found,
but you're the one who must look around.

So spend the time, enjoy the view.
It just might bring you life anew.

Merle Roehr

I awoke early to write this. I thought of the first verse as I was waking, it was four A.M., but as I sit and rewrite this piece, I am drinking coffee warmed in a microwave oven and eating English muffins with cream cheese. We have surely come a long way, yet sometimes I believe we have lost so much.

Wonderful, Beautiful Dawnin

Up before chuck an watchin the mornin.
Ain't it a wonderful, beautiful dawnin?
Tha critters a crawlin an smellin tha mornin.
Ain't it a wonderful, beautiful dawnin?
Tha cattle a millin, tha mournin dove cooin
Ain't it a wonderful, beautiful dawnin?
Mister sun a crackin up oer tha mountains.
Ain't it a wonderful, beautiful dawnin?
Tha smell o tha coffee, tha sizzelin o bacon.
Ain't it a wonderful, beautiful dawnin?
Tha cooks stirin camp, we're saddlin hosses.
Ain't it a wonderful, beautiful dawnin?
Gods givin a thick coatin of freshenin frostin.
Ain't it a wonderful, beautiful dawnin?

A Cowboy's Thoughts

With new hope an a prayin, lookin off in the distance.
Ain't it a wonderful, beautiful dawnin?
Gods givin tha time of lookin an xpectin.
Ain't He givin a wonderful, beautiful day?

Merle Roehr

Fences

Fences are one of those things that have come to be, through what has been called modernization. I am not so lost in time, but that I know they were necessary. Yet I often wonder if they were not just built out of power, greed, and control. I've built many a fence, and count it as enjoyable. As one who wishes to be lost in the mid 18 hundreds, they are simply boundaries and lost experiences. As I stand here on one side of the fence, I stare at the open beauty of no fences.

A Cowboy's Thoughts

The sign says no trespassing, do not enter, closed to the public, simply put no access.

No Access

As I stand and look at that old fence,
it seems to say "come on in."
The gate's standing wide open,
saying "welcome."
But standing there in the middle,
a big ol cedar.
It seemed as if to say,
"don't you enter."

There used to be a time,
when that land belonged to all men.
And the ol sign read
"welcome, come on in."
Take care of it on your way through,
The beauty that remains is up to you.
But now the fences their gates all locked.
Say "no access, not for you."

> There are those of us who would
> roam as the wind.
> There are those places that say,
> "welcome, come on in."
> But for some reason, there in the gate.
> The sign says, "no access, you'll have to wait."

We have owned, possessed, and wanted that which is not ours, until we face every gate all saying, "no access." I am assuming these things, have to do with the times. But I wish we were not, quite so blind.

I think that those who own, those who love, and those who abuse that beauty, have forgotten it was given by God. In essence our callousness stands in the gates of life saying,

"NO ACCESS"

Open Country

My dad and grandad were both cowhands, and many a story in my youth made me long for the days of old. The horses, cattle, and the open air. Still, nothing is as good or as real as the real thing. I've spent many days in the saddle now, and have continued in other endeavors. I now ride herd on several children, but my heart still longs to be saddled up and loose in big country. I love to see the creation, the rough-hewn canyons, the majestic mountains, the noise they make yet the quietness and comfort of them. The small creatures scurry and scatter about with their everyday habits so easily that I can't help but see the majesticness of my Lord and God. The feeling of comfort as if His arms were about me. To be able to visit with Him, to understand so much about Him, and remember His words. It makes me want to thank Him for placing the longing to be loose in my heart. I believe this is part of what makes me want to belong and be tied to God and His work in the kingdom.

Merle Roehr

Open Country

These fences we've built,
they separate us,
they confine us,
they control every thing in their presence.
There was a time they were hated.
Mostly by men much like me.
They wanted only to be free.
They wanted to experience and explore.
In some ways just to take it all in was enough.
Instead, they just felt cheated.
Not looking for anything important to most men,
only a necessity to be free.
Not for the reward that most seek,
but only for the rare beauty he sees.
There was no separation.
There were no boundaries,
only open country and places to see.
A man doesn't want much here at the end of the day,
just a place to graze a horse,
a plate of beans,
a cup of coffee
and a place to lay his head.

Home Range

It's good to be
on one's home range.
It's calm and safe
there's no need for change.
The world there
is peaceful and quiet.
There's no need
to show our might.
The world is out there
and we might not care.
But we're not looking
at what we must share.
We believe we have all we need,
but to their power we must heed.
The worlds advancement
is bound to climb,
and we don't care
to be left behind.
Now with the world,
we must grow,
but to home range
I'll always go.

Merle Roehr

A Place

I'm just a cowboy,
looking for a place to lay my head.
Some where beneath
that big blue sky.
Where it's beauty is there
laid open wide.
It's enough to make you sigh.

There's nothing there to crowd you in,
when with the coyote you lie.
I'm not sure it can still be done
but there are always those who try.

They do their best.
They work and they long,
but there's always someone to pry.
There's someone or something ever there.
It's enough to cause you to cry.

A Cowboy's Thoughts

Things I've Learned # 3

In my experiences as cowhand and afterwards,
and in hearing others talk of their experiences,
I have come to a couple of conclusions.
If I am presented with any bed,
including a roll on the ground, I can sleep.
The other thing I have experienced is,
that it is nearly impossible,
to enjoy or work in another's saddle.
It may be as personal as my underwear.

I have heard it said all my life,
I've found it to be in working with stock.
It takes months to put weight on stock.
But run them,
it takes only minutes to take it off.

We do a lot of beating around the bush,
when we need and want to bare our soul,
even to a friend.
We are a lot like the ol dog,
looking for a place to lie down.

He'll dig and paw around in a circle,
before he lays down.
We sometimes see this as comical,
But in a lot of ways he's a lot like us.
We're all looking for a place,
that's comfortable and safe.

Why is it we think we know a great deal about a subject?
When all we've dealt with is one episode within the subject.
They're some who would call it pride,
others call it stupidity.
Whatever it is called, it's a mistake.
Let those who really know about the subject,
deal with the discussing or teaching.
If they are wrong, then they are responsible.

We have heard it said
the first liar doesn't have a chance.
But sometimes the truth is funnier
than those things we make up.

If true life was boring,
no one would like it.

Careful Not to Kick the Wrong Cat, Better Yet Don't Kick the Cat at All

Back in the mid-eighties, I took a job on a ranch in the lower parts of the Palo Duro Canyons in the lower panhandle of Texas. The place laid between the small towns of Floydada, Matador, and Silverton, Texas. We called the place the horse pasture where we lived, but the good folks of that large city of Flomot, somewhere between 20 and 40, called the place rattlesnake ridge. Not a name known to my wife or me at the time. We did understand the name however, in the first sixty days. The time was late in the summer and anywhere between six feet of the porch and one mile, I killed about 90 rattlesnakes, hence the name. It doesn't sound much like we are talking about cats, but sure enough folks, we are talking lots of cats!

I had always heard where there are snakes there are mice and rats, sure enough there were, but that's a different story. Anyhow I determined that if there were enough cats the mouse population would decline, and maybe, just maybe, the snakes would just move out a little further from the house, thus the cats. I enlisted some friends and a few relatives in finding a few cats to work on the problem. I did not know that my problem was just starting. As you know, most small towns have too many loose cats. With the few people I had recruited to find cats, most told everyone they knew. The idea was, if you have a cat that's unwanted, Merle wants it! Just drop them off at the old barn. As you know, it's easier to start something than it is to stop it, sure enough the cat hunt was the same. Every day there were new cats showing at the barn, I was getting quickly overloaded. I had also expressed a need for all the cats to be somewhat wild, but I soon found out all unwanted cats are wild to someone else.

Now the story starts to get to the point, if the cats aren't wild it's time to make them that way. The first plan, don't feed the cat, thus they have to find mice (sounds right). It didn't work. You see I had a couple of ol dogs that I had decided would keep the cats off the porch, one was the worst porcupine killer I had ever seen and the other was an Aussie, Rottweiler cross that weighed close to eighty pounds. I assumed the small one would hate cats with the same passion as porcupine and the big one would keep all the food cleaned up. Wrong again, I found one dog licking the cats and the less food put out the more the dogs left for the cats. Next step, I decided if the dogs wouldn't scare them off I would. The idea was that each morning just a little before day breaks I stepped out on the back porch and proceeded to have an ol fashioned cat kicken. All the hard work seemed to be paying off, but as always no matter how well something works there are always problems. Seems there were about four big ol yearling kittens that somebody's kids must have made pets, cause no matter how hard you tried they were always there crawling on the screen or eating

A Cowboy's Thoughts

dog food, one of which was a black and white tom, starting when the kitchen light came on.

Well, we were getting late in the fall of the year, I had cleaned up quite a few of the barns, limited the mice, rattlesnakes were scarce, and the cats, there were always the cats! We were in the time of roundup and weaning yearlings, the days were long and hard, and the mornings were early. One of these mornings I was getting ready to go, making a pot of good ol black coffee, the waking up walking kind of cup of coffee, and the cats started to crawl on that porch screen. Being tired, sleep still in my eyes, and just a little more than irritated, I flung the back door open and started kicking that ol black and white tom. The ol cat hit the ground about thirty feet off the back porch and came running back. I decided I would cure his problem so I met him at the steps. Just as my foot connected, I caught out of the corner of my eye, the black and white tom curled up with that ol mean dog. I then realized that what I had kicked was not that ol tom, but one of the biggest pole cats (skunk) I had ever seen. Somehow I survived the event without the slightest aroma on my person, but I can't say as much for the porch and back yard. It seems we lived with it several days.

Seems the problem got better with the amount of cats. Some of them left, some stayed at the barn, but there were dogs, cats, and sometimes even a pole cat all curled up asleep on the porch together. The cat kicking never did work, in fact, it never occurred after this incident. One thing I learned. Be careful not to kick the wrong cat, better yet just don't kick the cat at all.

We all have many cats in life, we refer to them as problems. They come in many shapes and forms, but they are all still cats. From this experience in my life, let me give you one piece of advice.

DON'T GO AROUND KICKING THE CATS IN LIFE; IT JUST WON'T HELP.

Corky the Cat

This story is not politically correct, nor is it considered humanely acceptable by those in society who might consider ranch life and cowboys as barbarous. The situation is however true to life and realistic. Those who don't agree with this way of life I would not condemn, but I would never expect them to understand. I never knew a cowboy who didn't love his animals, and give them better care than most people. Their ways are just different.

You would have to realize what kind of cat Corky was. He was in fact a rather self indulged and brazen house cat. His origin had been, what you might call unacceptable. As I understand it, his momma had belonged to a woman of distinction, who carried this particular registered momma cat around with her. The cat had somehow escaped this lady's attention and gallivanted with the local ranch tom cats. One of these old toms was half Manx, the other half quite unknown. He had extra toes on each foot, not an uncommon trait of the cats in that part of the country. Anyhow the lady considered the momma cat socially unacceptable and refused to take her back. As for the tom cat, he was considered and very much so, to be of mixed blood, which would explain the features of ol Corky.

Now ol Corky, even as a kitten was ugly and had acquired extra large front feet. His shoulders were about an inch and a half lower than his hips, giving him a look as if he were always walking downhill. We think of most cats' tails being graceful and smooth, but this cat, his was the ultimate in ugly, or maybe just disgraceful. The tail on this cat was twisted and kinked, somewhat like a mashed corkscrew, and at maximum length it would not have been over four inches long full grown, thus the name. The cat's ears were double tufted making them look overly large. He was a dark bright yellow tabby with gold yellow eyes. Anyhow the cowboy at that particular camp was trying to rid himself of the excess cats. Me, I seemed to be in need of a cat for the ranch house where I was living to rid it of rats and mice. I decided he would fit the bill, and my wife thought he was so ugly that he was cute, we took him. Even as ugly as he was, there came to be quiet a fondness for him.

By the time he was a year old we came to find out that he possessed none of the qualities for which I had brought him home for. The rats I had wanted him to take care of did not frequent the house too often, but when they did there was no doubt they were there! You could be asleep at night and there would come the most horrible noises out of the kitchen ever heard. There was even one night that we had a rat skipping across the kitchen cabinet that was somehow able to knock a gallon coffee pot off the edge of the cabinet. It was empty, but even so it seems quite a feat, and becomes very disturbing in the dark of night. The only occasion I remember that cat deciding to fulfil his obligation to rid the house of rats was somewhat the same, and late at night. It sounded a little like someone rolling the washing machine around the kitchen. By the time I was finally able to convince myself to roll out of bed the noise had ceased, but only for a moment. About the time I thought all was quiet, that poor ol tom let out a blood curdling squall that I didn't even know a cat had the ability to make. Needless to say, by that time I had become quite concerned. When I finally found the light switch to the kitchen, ol Corky was in the opposite corner from that washer, watching it with a desperate look. He just sat there and looked, and ever once in a while he would let out a deep kinda growl. After that night he refused to go to his food or water until we moved it away from the washer. Now I might have held all this against that ol cat, but somehow my mind was changed. Now as an after thought for those who are familiar only with pet rats, I later caught this rat in one of those snapping rat traps. The trap caught him right at the base of the tail, and somehow hung under that old washer. When I finally figured out what I had, I was a little afeared myself. I finally killed him with a long mop handle. The rat himself not counting the tail was a little over a foot long and weighed near as much as that cat. I thought it unusual but later found out there were many nests all around the edge of the cap-rock with the same type rats. Needless to say the cat was no defense, and he decided to leave them alone.

Then there were the mice. The cat might have been hard in the head, but the heart was a different matter. I had watched him catch mice, but I had never seen him kill one. There had never been any doubt what Corky was doing with them. We supposed he was letting nature take it's coarse, and filling his belly. Wrong again, he would catch one of those mice and play with it in those big front paws. We watched him one day for an hour and with all those claws I never saw him expose one. In that whole time as he wallowed that mouse in his mouth I never saw any blood. You'd thought he was smooth mouthed. In about an hour and a half he grew tired and turned that mouse loose. That little mouse trotted off like nothing ever happened, both acted as if it were a game they played every day. Needless to say he weren't much use with the mice either, only to keep em company.

Within those two years, he seemed to become more possessive of his toys even the ones that belonged to my two-year old daughter. He even took to taking hold of her and expressing his opinions. Now my wife was usually easy going when it came to the cats, seemed she liked them. Then there was that spring day when Corky got a little carried away and scratched my daughter's face. My wife being very direct and very expressive, saw a vaquero that I worked with and me out the back door. The door burst open, and when I looked up she had that cat held up by the nap of the neck. She then slung that yellow ball of fur across the yard hollering "cut em or kill em." For those unaccustomed to the ranch slang, she was saying "I want him neutered or put to death." The two of us always up for a challenge, had been working cattle, so what's the big deal, we ranch work a cat, right!!! Oh, we got the cat working done. We had more cuts and scrapes on us than if a runaway horse had drug us through a mesquite thicket. Well, it seems ol Corky didn't think much of us for a few days, but he decided he would forgive us if he were going to get back in the house, and it sure did calm him down.

Now as I said, all cowboys love their animals and we had all become very fond of that ol cat. Oh, he was ugly as sin and we didn't get the work out of him we had expected, but you couldn't help but like him. Sometime a couple of years later that cat came down with a condition that was considered to be one that would become worse and incurable. There are

A Cowboy's Thoughts

always decisions to be made that none of us like, but being a realistic person I knew what must be done. I met my wife at the door one day at lunch, she had ol Corky in her arms and tears in her eyes. He had become worse and unable to walk, we decided there was no use in him hurting. I went to the bedroom to get my twenty-two, trying to think of how to tell a five-year-old what was happening. Now she had grown up as most children on a ranch do. She realized that you hunt to eat, and this particular incident had never crossed her mind. The tears were something she wasn't understanding.

Now we all seem to get over grief one way or another, and this cat's life had always been comical in many ways. It kinda seemed appropriate that there came humor in the time of his death to help us through it. There are those who might take this the wrong way, so let me clear it up. Death is never funny, not even if I am killing for food or protection for my stock. All life is precious but death in reality comes to all things and sometimes I am involved, and sometimes it hurts. We all need ways of relieving that hurt. So here it is, in a five-year old's eyes. In all sincereness and in all of her innocence, she looks at me with that cat and that twenty-two and posed this question. "Momma, we eat Corky?" Any death is not funny, not even in our animals but it is real, we must deal with it. Oh, we laughed at what she said, right then and there and then every time afterward that we remembered her thought. Deal with it; we did.

Merle Roehr

Giving Up the Horses

Seems like I've been away from the ranch a long while now. I have always been one to be just a tad sentimental, I always keep reminders. Like most cowboys it's hard not to keep a horse, I have known several who did just that. At that time in my young life it sounded like such a waste of horseflesh, just standing around. We're funny like that, youth is sometimes so uncaring and ignorant. I remember an older woman who worked with my wife in a flower shop, she called it "young and dumb." Well, anyhow it's been nice to keep a few horses along the way. Some might have even been considered fairly good. No matter their looks and disposition they have always connected me with that life I find enjoyable.

Now all of us know that horses are big animals, for the most part. We also know they are creatures that need quite a lot of discipline, something that takes time. Time which most of us don't have. It is also a fact that we must keep ourselves in shape and disciplined as well, this too takes much time. I realized a while back, I might have missed both of these points. I had not taken the time for my horses or for me. As a result I have found myself taking a great deal

A Cowboy's Thoughts

of time to heal. It seems that 270 pounds does not bounce well, and that older men's bodies don't take the abuse they did when young.

I was trying to keep five or six horses in line, all at the same time trying to care for the work I was hired for. That job description did not have a use for the horses, even though they were a part of my relaxation and were good therapy for the children we were working with. I even felt a little guilty, in that I wasn't teaching them anything. As always the job became more consuming and the horses became less. I still loved the horses, or at least what they stood for to me. Oh, I still enjoyed the riding but I would find myself forgetting to do something, or I would not read my mount for what he was telling me. I would find myself sometimes having a difficult time getting in the saddle. Most of these things were caused by the horse being out of practice and me being too out of shape.

Seems we had a sorrel gelding that was "pet broke," and had never given any problems. We would saddle him and let the children ride, always without incident. We had decided to take the children down on that day to ride. I had that day forgotten how important it was to prepare and pay attention to my surroundings. I had curried the ol gelding out, without problems. I saddled him up and watched him stomp around and flinch as I cinched him up, it never occurred to me there might be something wrong. I would have always walked him out, let him relax, but I just didn't see the use that day. I always rode him before I let the children on and that day was no different, other than I just led him out the gate and stepped upon him. Not paying attention to him laying his ears back, I didn't even get set in the saddle. That ol pet busted into. He took eight or ten jumps in a hundred and fifty feet. About that time I did a tumble over the other front shoulder, landing flat of my back. All I could do was watch all four feet come right over my face. It took me a great while to be able to rise to my feet, seems my breath was gone, a few ribs broke and some mighty big bruises began to show. I did finally get to my feet and catch that ol gelding. I believe he was as scared as I was. He didn't have a clue what he'd done. Of course the children liking rodeos, thought they had just seen a bronc rider. Seems they decided that if I could stay six or seven seconds without being in the saddle I just might be good. I didn't have the heart to relate the fear or the pain to them. I did finally get him into the round pen, pulled the saddle and saddled him again. In the process I found what that ol pet was trying to tell me all the time "cactus spines under the cinch were mighty uncomfortable" in more than one way. Well It took all I had but I climbed back on that ol pet and worked him around then let the kids ride. I knew then there were more horses than time, and there just wasn't enough use for them.

I still couldn't bring myself to give em up. After two months of healing time, I saddled a little mare I had. She was nice enough, and had been easy going, she was even started on bits. After working her while I realized she wasn't responding to the bits the way she should. My mind told me to take her to the barn and put a hackamore on her, but I kept telling myself she'd come around. I brought her up the slope and when she saw daylight, I'm guessing something spooked her. She broke into an uncontrolled run. Not something a fat, out of practice cowhand necessarily needs. Needless to say she didn't answer to the bits. Now somewhere along the way I realized she was headed for a gully full of concrete. I decided it was more honorable to bail than to land in that gully. It still hurt mightily.

A Cowboy's Thoughts

Well, to come to the end, I was quite devastated. Not because I had been spilled twice in two months, rather I had just realized that I was no longer in my youth and I was suddenly full of fear. Not afraid of the horses but afraid of mortality. I have several friends who just wouldn't give em up. Some are just stove up, some stay in practice, and there are a couple who are in a wheelchair for life. Don't get me wrong, we must all do what we must do, and we all have our price to pay. What took me two or three weeks of healing as a young man has taken me over a year now. I decided to get rid of most of the horses. It just seemed to me if I were out of shape and practice, and the horses were out of practice, and the communication was not between us, there was not much good would come of it. Now I might have needed to get rid of all the horses, but I just couldn't. You see they have become a part of my life. It's just too hard to see them go at this time. The two that are left don't get rode much. They are there to put a hand on and to push me around. Besides, I never did find a law that said a horse has to be ridden. I don't feel guilty any more and I still enjoy having them around. I am sure there is a young man out there who looks at me and my horses and thinks "what a waste of horseflesh." Not at all.

Merle Roehr

Slopping Horses

It happens that in about 1992, I left the good ranch and farm country of West Texas. We moved to the high mountain desert, and began to live a lifestyle that was much different. We had taken on the work of caring for children who were not as fortunate as others in life. Most were in need of just having a loving family. This type of life leaves you in some different circumstances than most, it becomes necessary for you to depend on others for your support and living. Among one of the most important things you can bring with you besides God, is life's experiences. You learn to give as many as you can to them and hope it gives them a head start, just as you would your own.

Now as for me, mine were vast, but were still very limited to my ranch and farm culture, so these were what I used. Animals and plants have always been good teaching material for life, so I have acquired a great many of both. The facility with which I had accepted a position functioned on many donations. Much of the food was through these donations, some were in bulk and had to be sorted through. We would receive a load of apples or potatoes and they would be in excess or there would be a large amount that

A Cowboy's Thoughts

might be well past prime. When they had been sorted through there was always waste just to be thrown away. For some reason, most likely from being raised on the farm, I just couldn't throw them away. I had learned that nearly anything could be used as feed for one animal or another. At the time of the apples and potatoes and even some onions, I had purchased a few head of Nubian and Boar goats for show for 4-H. Seems they did very well on this type of diet, with the small cost of a supplement. Funny they seemed to really like the onions. Didn't do much for the milk though. I remember even receiving several tons of whole corn one year. We decided to buy a couple of old scrub cows to fatten out, seemed everyone laughed. I had learned when spending time working for a feedlot, that at least 50 percent of feedlot beef was older stock. I figured the same way I had with the goats, a little supplement would carry the corn a long ways. For some reason people quit laughing when we started eating T bone steaks for less than a dollar a pound. Seems they were pretty good.

Along with this extra food the one thing I had not expected was the governments' dislike for the use of canned goods, which were past expiration dates. The oddest point was that not one man of them, could tell you why. All I ever got "that's just the way it is." I seemed to have a lot of it. Most was as good as the day it was canned. We had to do something with it, but that wasn't good enough for me. Somewhere along the way I had a lot of goods to trash. Now I had been raised slopping hogs and feeding grain to make good bacon, so I decided to start feeding hogs, it made good pork. Well it doesn't matter what you do someone will find something wrong with it. Seems the government has a little something against feeding slop to hogs. Now that bothered me just a little, It seemed to me the hogs really liked it and they were all healthy enough to butcher.

Now I had become just a little more than worried about the waste and the over concerns of our government. I decided that I could feed out my own pigs and be at least lawful and not waste what was considered not fit for use. Now I have known of a few old wagon cooks who have affectionately fed their mounts sourdough biscuits. I would not try to out do their affection, I simply refused to waste anything that could be fed. I started to realize that my hog pens looked as though someone had tried to run through them, but had found no reason. The pens were in the middle of the horse lots, so I always fed the horses first and everything else afterwards, finishing with the hogs ten gallons of slop. Well I had started to clean out some of the surplus when I took over food services and found eight or nine large boxes of pizzas that someone had given us. I decided that the kids would enjoy so I took several home. When we unpackaged them, we found that they were two crusts pressed together, There was a little cheese for topping along with large lumps of something. I had left them to thaw for the night and when they reached room temperature, we found that those lumps of something were mold. Now I have three hundred pounds of moldy pizzas. I have always fed horses good grain and good hay, but for some reason I dumped a box of those pizzas in the hay bunk. To my surprise you would have thought I had filled that bunk with good grain and molasses. I didn't seem to have any problems ridding myself of the pizzas. Well those hog pens were still going down and I still didn't know why. There was a fence behind the barn that was in bad need of repairs so I decided to work it into shape after feeding. There began to be a great deal of squealing in the hog pens, more than I usually heard. I stepped around the barn and there leaning on those hog panels was a sorrel gelding with his teeth latched onto one of those ol hogs' neck. I decided it wasn't anything to be concerned about until I finished. Well it wasn't but a few minuets till I heard the worst noise, the squealing was as bad as I had ever heard, with the sound of hooves flaying against those hog troughs. When I rounded the corner there were three horses that had fell plumb over that panel. Now I had three horses and two hogs fighting over one trough with the slop that was left in it. The funniest sight was watching that ol sorrel horse trying to drag one of those hogs off the trough by his ear and that ol hog flopping his head back and forth squealing, trying to get away.

Now that the mystery of the fence was found, the cure was also found. Simple, just change the feeding procedure. The hogs were about ready to go to market so I decided to scatter four of those hog troughs through the horse lots. I would give the hogs five gallons of slop then split another ten gallons between the troughs for six horses. Now I never had much fight among those horses, but I found out that they would all rather have four ounces of slop than a whole bucket of good grain. Besides, something had to eat the slop.

Merle Roehr

Live Life

When you turn a good horse
loose on a wild cow
in an old mesquite thicket.
Be sure you're ready to follow.

This idea comes from first hand experiences. It's not that they were planned, they just occurred. Nevertheless they have given me good tools to use in life. It seems that in one of these instances we were gathering cattle off a place we were going to lease out. The company that was leasing insisted that there was not to be one head of stock left, for fear that their purebred program would be disrupted. The company I was working for kept good stock but, there was a great deal of Longhorn and Brahma mixed in. They were always considered good stock and always topped the market when we sold yearlings. As always, there is wild stock, but we managed to always rid ourselves of trouble makers. Now we were moving all the stock into a trap to give us time to wean older calves and give the younger ones time to pair up with their mamas. As we came closer, I noticed there were several head of scrub bulls over a year old and

A Cowboy's Thoughts

two or three long heifers, a situation that should not have happened, If the man who had been caring for the stock had been tending to business, but that's another story. Any how I had been watching one of these heifers for a good while and had figured that the more closed in she felt the wilder she would become. I had been giving her plenty of room, but the trap was near and it became necessary to push just a little harder. Now there really wasn't much place to go once we got passed an old mesquite thicket. Let me explain this thicket. It was much like all other thickets in that part of the country. It had been killed out about forty years before and had been an old thicket then, with brush being in some places thirty and forty feet high. All of this was indeed dead and standing, now with new growth that was ten to fifteen feet tall. Now all things considered, we were doing well. The boss had been using the horn on the pickup to call the cattle and another man and I were bringing up the rear a horse back with about two-hundred fifty head of grown stock. We were using the thicket for a blind until we hit the angle fence. The boss had parked the pickup in the road just out of sight on the other side of the thicket. Well all about the same time this heifer saw the pickup and a hole in the thicket. I saw her head go up, the boss had jumped out of the pickup screaming, "don't let her get away." Now as you can guess that heifer got just a little more than excited. She found that hole in that thicket. It was before I realized what I was doing that I turned a horse that stood seventeen hands tall and a man weighing two-hundred fifty pounds loose on a heifer going through a four-foot hole in that thicket. Now all I remember after that point, was throwing my forearms up in front of me, ducking my head and thinking I might have made a mistake. Only thing I knew, it was too late to stop that ol sorrel horse. His mind was made up and I wouldn't jump. You see, even if it didn't look too promising coming out the other side of this half mile of thicket, it was gonna be fun. Well I did come out, it was fun and I did pay. My forearms looked as if someone had beat them with a big stick. I did feel lucky there was a four-inch limb wedged under the saddle horn, the horse didn't have a scratch on him and I collected that ol heifer. My boss had been thinking the same thing when I turned that horse loose. When the dust cleared he was coming back down that road looking for a horse. I questioned his presence. The only response I ever received was he was seeing where the horse came out so he could come find me. Now I am not sure where the line is, that danger should be avoided, but I do know that in life there are dangers to be faced. Some have to be faced with snap decisions and some are confronted with thought, but all will be decided upon. The one thing I do know, each of us live only once.

If you don't pursue
all things in life
with a passion.
You only half live the life.

Working Rough Stock

Now in youth there are things that are done that seem to be right. There also comes a time as we mature that they are considered cruel and even a little unintelligent. I'm not sure why we do these things, whether out of frustration, anger, revenge or self defense. Oh, one other thing, it might be something that just has to be done.

Now at one time or another all cowboys have had to gather and work stock in less than desirable situations and conditions. This is where most of these events stem from. These situations and conditions are there most often because someone did not do a thorough job or nature is in extreme. It doesn't make a difference what the profession is, there are those who want to do things the easy way, even in cow work.

The first two events are not events that I had the advantage of being involved in. It took place in the fifties and was a story I heard growing up from my dad, he being a JA's cowboy. It also may not fit the pattern, but was an ending of an era. Even though the ranch handled purebred stock there was still a scattering of stock considered unfit for good stock. The times were also changing, the need for

Merle Roehr

the stock to be better and the cowboys not quite so wild, the world called it progress. Now as usual when stock are run in rough country over a great amount of time you accumulate a fair amount of wild stock. Now some of this just happens, some was caused by not gathering well or just letting stubborn stock drop back, anyhow it was there. It had taken a fair amount of mighty good cowboying and a great amount of time to gather most of this wild stock. As always toward the end the frustrations set in. There were those that had to be gathered with a rope and time, always the wildest and most determined. So, you might think fifteen head in a hundred sections was no big deal. One problem was, most were bulls and mixed with purebreds, produced trash. The other problem is that bulls are creatures with their own mind and they intend to use it. Now if it were told right, they used burros as lead animals after the bulls were caught. When I say caught, I mean that there where several cowboys who rope an old bull, took him down, cut him, and then sawed the horns off, leaving only stubs. They would then tie a rope around the horns then tie the other end up short, in a squar knot in with that burro's tail, seems the knot would not slip, then they would turn them loose to head home. Now you might need to understand, the burro had more mind than the bull and after he kicked that ol bull in the nose the first hour or so then he'd lead him to the house. Something about sweet feed had a powerful pull on that burro. Another fact, stock that is genuinely wild fights, or when it is downed decides to die and die it does. Now a lot of them died just because they wanted to, a few of them were lead in, and some fought to kill. In this particular instance there was a big ol bull that one of the cowboys roped while still in a dead run. When the cowboy shoved his horse up close beside him, the ol bull slung his head at the horse. Well this ol bull had a righteous set of horns, one of which caught that horse right in the juggler vein. Needless to say the horse was dead for three or four steps, still in a dead run, before he hit the ground. The horse rolled heels over head over the cowboy, easy way for a cowboy to die. The man was actually blessed, in that he was able to take his saddle and ride off on another horse. This story just lets you know just how dangerous an old bull and a good set of horns are, and maybe why a man can become so frustrated.

Now the next event, they were still gathering wild stock, when a maverick bull broke the herd and caught an old horse in the belly with his horns and ripped him open. Either the horse wasn't fast enough or maybe he just didn't have enough sense. Nevertheless, the horse was dead in his tracks. Now I can't say what the reasoning was behind the next move, I wasn't there, but I have given you the options that I see might fit. These men somehow accomplished the task of roping that ol bull and taking him down. They cut him, and my guess was with a dull knife. It could have been the cook's butcher knife. Then one of them produced the camp axe and proceeded to relieve him of his horns, leaving him with about six inches of bloody jagged stumps. Now these days that might seem mighty rough, but I'm told he followed the wagon home.

Now it was some thirty years later that I found myself on a working ranch in the rough country of the lower Palo Duro Canyons. The old man I worked for had informed me of the neighbor's stock running on our land. Now understand, he was a good neighbor but if the advantage was there he would take it. In other words he would open the water gaps, shove his stock through and then put the gap back up or if the gap washed out he didn't bother putting it back up at all. I would usually return them in the same manner or pen them and

Merle Roehr

trailer them back home. I had always been taught to be fairly neighborly, it seemed to always pay off. The only problem is, when an ol cow learns the grass is better, she's bound to find the way herself. Now I had begun to have trouble with several, but one ol cow in particular. She was a high-headed, crooked horned, ugly, Hereford. She was always on the prod, and she always meant business. I had gathered her on six or eight occasions and upon returning her, the old man always swore he was sending her to packers. The problem was when I left he turned her out the back gate. She seemed to always beat me back to the bottom side of our place. Well it seems the last time I caught her, I found myself on her business side of a good fight. I survived the incident but my shirt and trousers were not quite so lucky. I was finally able to put her in the loading chute, but I soon found that she had managed to jar a gate loose and was in the working ally. Try as I might, she refused to back out, she ended up in the squeeze chute and halfway out the side. I managed to squeeze the chute down and put the bars in place, but she wasn't going to budge. Now I was trying to decide what I might be able to do to rectify the situation. There was for some reason a broad bladed hatchet always stuck in a post at the corner of the chute, and today was no different. When I turned around there it was, now I had been aggravated, run over and abused. I jerked that hatchet from the post and in about four solid licks, surprise, dehorned. Needless to say it did not improve her looks. To my surprise when I took her home, the only response I received from the old man was "my lord son, you ruined her" I never saw her again. Now I don't know if I would have ever dehorned her in this manner if I had never heard the story, but it worked.

It was a short time after this event, that the old man had a Shorthorn, Longhorn cross bull with the same type problem. Although we didn't dehorn him, the cure still had an effect on his horns. He had a tremendous set of horns, but they just were not very long. The vaquero I worked with had his own kind of cure. His idea was for me to push him down the fence line. I was to keep him between the fence and the bumper of the pickup on the passenger's side, keeping him in a run. Now he believed if I held the bull straight, He could take a small twenty-two caliber rifle that I always carried and unload it in that ol bull's horns. Now he was right, after about sixteen rounds that ol bull plunged through that six-wire fence like a swarm of hornets had hit him. Now as I look back, it must have presented tremendous pain, for the bellowing was awful each time lead burrowed into those horns. As I said before it might not have been what most folk claim acceptable behavior, but it was mighty effective. We never saw the bull south of the fence again and he always viewed us, at a distance.

Now there were several other occasions of this type that have happened in my life on the ranch. It is also often, no matter how others see these things, that there is a certain amount of humor in them. Now the response of the man, and the bellowing of the bull was and has become rather humorous even though I would hope maturity would make me think of a better way to achieve the same results. There is however one last occasion that the memory always brings, at least a smile. We had been told that most of the ranch had been leased and that it must be cleaned. The ranch had been blessed, at one time, with a man who had the habit when gathering stock, to just drop off the bulls if they were not needed or if they decided they just didn't want to be brought in. Most of the country we were gathering had a few Longhorn, Hereford cross bulls that stayed in the breaks. They had been there longer than any of the stock

Merle Roehr

and had become quite accustom to staying behind. They were, determined to stay put. The old man on the outfit had determined to hire young cowboys, some who were wild but experienced to gather the bulls that had not been brought in. They had been able to gather all but one ol bull that had decided to take up residence on the back corner in a mesquite thicket, way back up in a canyon. Now one of these boys was a pretty good cowboy and owned a big sorrel saddle horse. Both had some experience with bulls and had been raised in rough country. He decided to just bring that ol bull out of that thicket. The ol bull had no intention of leaving and refused to budge until he was able to run one of those horns through that horse's flanks. It didn't seem to hurt the horse too bad, but the cowboy had to walk him back to camp and the horse never was the same around cattle. Now the old man decided to bring the ol bull in and I would have to give him credit, he did it by himself. As I said the ol bull was determined to stay, but what was funny he was almost a pet, he would take grain cubes from your hand. Well the old man took a logging chain and tied it to a good green mesquite stump and started to feed that ol bull by hand, one cube at a time. Somewhere in the process he laid that chain looped over that ol bulls horns. I would like to have been a cottontail rabbit watching from the bushes, there seemed to be plenty of action, I will say there was evidence of this fact, but the bull was still caught. Now the old man with a strong trailer, a good rope and a stout sorrel stud horse, loaded that bull. We must understand, this event, from the time the old man started, had lasted all day. I saw or more precisely heard them late that evening. They had shown up at the place I lived on, and anything that was shipped out was shipped from there so it was the logical place to bring him. Now what I heard sounded like

A Cowboy's Thoughts

a revved up Harley. When I peered around the barn, I'm not sure what was making the most noise, the bull bellowing or that old dull chainsaw rocking back and forth through those six inch horns. The sight of that ol bull with his horns chained to the front of that trailer, and the old man with that dull chainsaw and the blood which was not as much as it looked to be, was unforgettable. I was told not to turn that ol bull loose until it was on a shipper truck. He was for some reason mighty wild and his attention span was pretty short. I did however find out one day how to get his attention. I was cleaning a small mower and cranked it at the back of the barn, I suppose it sounded a bit like that chainsaw. He didn't seem to want to fight it, but he didn't want to turn his back on it either. It seems I could crank that mower and back that bull anywhere in that set of pens. Now I'm not saying that the things we did were good, correct, or even humane by most standards, but they worked. If you think my humor is somewhat twisted, close your eyes and watch a man with a small mower, back a twenty-five hundred-pound bull into a shipper's truck.

Merle Roehr

The Ending of Only a Beginning

It was late in the year 1988. There had been a number of tremendous happenings that year, a time of decisions, hurtful, and happy events. Of all the things, I was living a life in the fashion I had always dreamed of. The problem is we always come to a time in life when we must look at all the situations and options and move own with life. Now every event in life shapes and molds each of us, and in the manner we exist on any given day, these are the things that build or tear us down.

I am considered by some and am in normal circumstances, a large man, at just over six foot and two hundred-fifty pounds. Folks often see me as hard as a piece of rawhide, loud and gruff with a flamboyant touch. Most of these things cover an interior, in which emotions run deeper than an old mesquite grub, living on that wind blown, dried grassland of West Texas. It seems that these things have been brought about by many things, but there are two in particular. When I was young in life I was taken near death by an infectious disease and about the time this story takes place, I took myself to the point of death with my mental and emotional being. It does not make me weak or strong, it just brings out a difference in my way of seeing things as they happen in my life.

I had within this year seen my son born, my father had a severe heart attack and I had watched my family lose my attention because of the work load that had come about for other reasons. Seems no one was to blame, life just happens. Now it was not to say that I didn't enjoy the work. I was living a life that I had dreamed of since my childhood. I was a cowboy. It was not to say that the man I worked for was not a good man, he was one of the best I had ever known. All in all life was good, but at the time changes were necessary. In that this was the life I had always dreamed of, the turmoil was great. I had talked with the boss with much reluctancy and had made preparations for the change. I had decided to give the place one last going over, which would take the month. The man deserved the best in my going and I was going to give it.

The first two weeks of December were easy enough, and I spent most of my days on the more obvious things. There were barns to make sure were clean, checking the mills conditions and seeing that the traps and working pens were in good shape, they would all be needed in the spring. The last check on the calving heifers and the brood mares, to make sure that the pastures would carry them through was finished. There was still the daily feeding of the pastures that were on top of the cap-rock. That was a continual activity through Christmas, along with the bailing and stacking the last of this year's hay. These were the everyday tasks of ranch work, but I loved it, no matter the monotony of it. There was that last day just before the first of the year, which was the hardest. My wife and I had most everything ready to move and it was stacked in the middle of the house. Tonight I looked around the old ranch house, as odd as the setup was I couldn't imagine being anywhere else, much less the little farm house we were moving into. There was a wrap around sunroom with big french-doors opening into the livingroom. It was there you could stand of an evening with a cup of coffee and watch the sunset just below the edge of the cap-rock. Most evenings that would be feeding time, I could walk to the back side of the pens, climb upon the top rail and watch the sun set on the horizon across that old canyon. At that moment there were great anxieties for the next day.

Last night I had penned Little Rebel. He was my favorite horse. It wasn't that he was better than the others, and it wasn't because he was beautiful, cause he wasn't. As it was, that little horse had the biggest heart I'd ever seen. He just seemed to be the one horse that belonged there, and I wanted that last day to be on him. Now the morning was not an early morning but the frost was thick and everywhere. All the senses were heightened, the breath of the Rebel could be seen with every heave of his chest as he stood at the fence. The saddle creaked with every movement and the sunlight danced on every crystal of the frost. I knew the day would be long, but knowing that it would come to an end, made it forever too short. I saddled the Reb and walked him through that old heavy swinging gate, then through the pasture gate. I stood there for a great while, long enough that he seemed to question me. He always disliked me mounting up, but this morning he seemed to know the difference, I rode to the road going off the cap-rock, this had always been my favorite place. When I checked fences or water gaps my day started and ended here, just as it would today. The canyon was gray with the frosted cedar and carried that enhanced aroma. It was strong in my nostrils, so intense that as I think of it, my emotions long for that time. I just wanted to soak it all in, the view, the smells, the memories. If it could have been up to me that time could have been forever, but life goes on and I needed to put twenty-five miles in before the sunset.

It was more than two miles to the bottom of Hall Creek pasture and many memories had taken place in that two miles. At the top of the first rise there were always deer, this morning was no different. It just so happened that it was where I had shot my first one. The excitement still lingered as I watched the small bucks slip into the draws of the canyon and wait for me to move on. There were other things to draw my attention, the mill and tank opposite the draw was a place that we always stopped at as a family. It was one of those places, when you see a picture of a mill you think this has to be it. The mill, no matter the season it was always beautiful and full of enjoyment, maybe everything there just brought good memories. I suppose it was about being free and wild, where I wanted to be. By lunch I had checked the upper gaps and had made it to a set of falls on the creek. I had not brought anything as far as a meal, just a couple of biscuits and bacon, but it gave me time to set and enjoy the sounds and views of the falls. Oh they didn't make much noise but they seemed to scream for you to quench your thirst, the water was cool and sweet and always there. Further down the stream, fresh water was not always the case, but here, it was a promise and seemed every creature knew it. It was a place of seclusion and refuge for all, and today it was there for me. The scale of feelings ranged from the height of enjoyment of memories to the bottom of a pool of heartaches, of now letting go of this part of my dreams. Again this stream seemed to fill the soul with that refreshing feeling that was needed at this time. There were about ten gaps on the lower part of the place and not enough leisure time to set and enjoy if I were to finish before sunset. In fact I would need to ride pretty hard, and the Reb would indulge me. By the time I had returned to the picturesque mill the shadows were lengthening and the air was beginning to cool. I stopped, dismounted and put on the warmth of a jacket. There I let the Reb drink, and for the last time I took a long draw of the water from the mill myself. There were a few moments to look around, then mounting up, it was on up the hill to the house. Now it was about a mile to the house and only a quarter from the mill to the top. It seemed that the quarter to the top was the longest I had ever seen. I thought of all the last things I had seen and done. I loved the place, what it stood for and the way of life I had been able to enjoy, I would miss it. The tears of sadness streamed down my face all the way up the hill, I didn't pay much attention to Reb, he knew the way. He turned out of the road and toward the house. When I looked up, I saw my wife standing on the back porch, I knew she was thinking some of the same things. This was my last ride up that hill and this was the last time they would watch me ride in. My daughter was, as always, hollering "daddies coming" and dancing all over the porch. My wife was smiling but the tears were there, she would miss it too. I remembered the first days, I think she thought she had been condemned. She had eventually found a love for it and knew I loved it too.

I dismounted and loosened the cinch so the Reb could breathe with ease, as usual he had just broken a good sweat, seems he was just as tough as his heart was big. I picked up my daughter and took my wife's arm, with the reins thrown over my shoulder and headed to the barn. I took the extra time with the Reb, in cleaning and brushing him dry, I then

A Cowboy's Thoughts

gave him a few extra oats, just my way of saying goodby. The chores done, my family and I stepped to the edge of the cap-rock and watched the sunset.

It's hard to say goodby to a way of life that is full of romance and one of love, but life goes on. I know that it has been good for my family and me, but I'll always long to be a cowboy, free and wild. It will always bring a tug at this old heart to think of those days, on that place in my life, but life, it's good. Now if the Good Lord brings the chance around again, I might just take it. If He doesn't offer it again, I've enjoyed it once. That is so much more than most men receive. I have lived my dream once, the sun has set and I have enjoyed.

Merle Roehr

End of the Line

Goodbye's

Here it is time to say goodbye
to friends that we have made.
They have been here just a short while,
but we're going to miss their smiles.

The time to part is always hard
for we've come close in these few days.
But realize we must they'll never be gone,
for the memories we have made.

And we knew when they came,
their intent was never to stay.
We've worked and laughed
we've played and prayed.

The time now to part has come.
So with all these things and all our fun
we are going to miss them so.
And so it is with God's good speed
we have bid them go.

This is dedicated to those who have come into our lives and into childcare. There will be an everlasting appreciation and thanks for all they have done. I will never remember all the names or faces. I will, however remember the acts of kindness and hard work, but most of all the friendships that have occurred. None of these things will be forgotten. Thanks

Thank You for Taking a Part of My Life

There are several concepts within this thought. To start with it is addressed to the cowman, cowboy, bronc rider, rodeo performer, clown, wind millers, the old cook or any others who can put themselves in this picture. We need to realize what we have been given in the life we have been able to live, and it's importance to others.

In this day and time when the cowboy seems to live in near extinction, one of the most intriguing things we have in this country is nostalgia. It also seems from my prospective that cowboy nostalgia is among the most popular. I believe the most significant reasons for this is the need of comfort and enjoyment of a slower pace of life, along with the thought of romance.

In my growing up, the cowboy was placed in many categories. Now as a working cowboy and what we thought to be the only kind of cowboy, we made the differences very wide. We called many so-called cowboys by names like cowboy wanna be, drug store cowboy, or rodeo cowboys. Now as I look back there are many ways to fulfill an objective. There are always little boys and most all of them want to be a cowboy sometime as they grow up. No, I may not approve of what they look like or whom they associate with. There were those in my growing up years that were so-called hippies and now we have those who are considered punkers. They do everything from team roping to bull riding and yes, even real cow work. This only confirms that now the cowboy is not a style, but who a man is inside.

I have talked to those who own what we used to call dude ranches and those who own real cow ranches who open them up to the public as places for working vacations. In most cases they are very well accepted by many Easterners and by those who live in large cities in this country. They see it as an opportunity to experience the life of the west, whether it is one of these things, a ride in a horse drawn wagon or a chuck wagon meal. Whatever the event is, many of us who have lived this type of life may have missed their point. We look at their lack of skills in this environment and are disappointed and sometimes mighty critical. Until recently I had not realized what was happening. These people, in our eyes ask questions and pester on an all time high. They return to their homes excited and overjoyed with the experience. They dress the part as best they know and present themselves as cowboys, we are amused by their efforts. There is though, one thing I have heard given by these individuals. There is always a big thanks. It is not, however, for the physical things they accomplish, but for being privileged to live a small part of our life and us bearing through it. The reason I have come to this conclusion, is because a cowboy I visited with told me, they just want a little bit of what we have. If anything, we as the cowboy, should be flattered.

A Cowboy's Thoughts

As I said earlier, the way of the cowboy seems to be under the threat of extinction. Oh the life of the cowboy can still be found, but not as easily as it was at one time. There are those who want to know about and experience it, they will be the ones to help keep it alive. As for those who live the life, please try to share it. For those who seek to live a small part through us, I must say from the heart of this cowboy: Thank You and Best Wishes.

Merle Roehr

Eventide

The moon rises full and bright.
The clouds float thin and light.

The pot of coffee,
been set to cool.
The fire flickering,
like the glistening pool
.
The only sounds,
are the coyote's howls.
The snort of a horse,
the lowing of the cow.

A time to meditate,
a time to pray.
Night has been set to rest,
it's time to lay.

About the Author

Merle Roehr was born and raised in West Texas. He was married in 1983, and they have two children. He was reared with a strong belief in God and family. He and his family moved to New Mexico in 1991, where they now work in child care. He is a cowman in every since of the word, by heritage, by experience and heart, right down to his eighteen inch green top boots.